PUNCH
NEEDLE

T0287069

PUNCH NEEDLE

Fifteen contemporary projects

Rachel Lawson
& Siobhan Watt

SCHIFFER
PUBLISHING

4880 Lower Valley Road · Atglen, PA 19310

Other Schiffer Books on Related Subjects:

Punch Needle Rug Hooking, Amy Oxford,
ISBN 978-0-7643-6015-2
Punch Needle Extravaganza, Laetitia Dalbies,
ISBN 978-0-7643-6258-3
Rug Hooking with Wool Strips, Katie Kriner,
ISBN 978-0-7643-6209-5

Library of Congress Control Number: 2021942727

Produced by BlueRed Press Ltd. 2021
Designed by Insight Design Concepts Ltd.
Type set in Fira Sans

ISBN: 978-0-7643-6319-1
Printed in India

Published by Schiffer Publishing, Ltd.
4880 Lower Valley Road
Atglen, PA 19310

Phone: (610) 593-1777; Fax: (610) 593-2002

Email: Info@schifferbooks.com
Web: www.schifferbooks.com

For our complete selection of fine books on this and related subjects, please visit our website at www.schifferbooks.com. You may also write for a free catalog.

Schiffer Publishing's titles are available at special discounts for bulk purchases for sales promotions or premiums. Special editions, including personalized covers, corporate imprints, and excerpts, can be created in large quantities for special needs. For more information, contact the publisher.

We are always looking for people to write books on new and related subjects. If you have an idea for a book, please contact us at proposals@schifferbooks.com.

Contents

Introduction

With its meditative rhythm, punch needle is a craft that is both simple to master and calming to do; you can let your hands create while your mind relaxes. The result is a profound sense of well-being, along with your own uniquely beautiful textile art.

This is a traditional rug-making craft and one that is totally accessible to everyone, including those with no craft experience. It is a delightful hobby to discover and a perfect way to turn a stash of yarn into practical items.

Growing up, Rachel and Siobhan enjoyed drawing and painting, heartily encouraged by their parents. It must be in their blood: their father built a successful business restoring secondhand furniture, and they admire the sculpture work of their relative Tommy Duncan, who lives and works as an artist in New York City.

After schooling, Siobhan went on to study art and completed a degree course in textiles and fashion design, specializing in screen printing. Creating artwork for screen printing means simplifying the design to produce a graphic that prints well—successful punch needle designs require this exact same eye for bold and simple artworks.

Crafting and creativity has long been a hobby for Rachel, and the inspiration for The Modern Crafter came about when Rachel asked Siobhan to design her something to punch-needle for relaxation while on maternity leave. Rachel loved the combination of Siobhan's bold artworks with the accessibility of punch needle, something she felt should be shared with others—we hope you agree.

Together, Siobhan and Rachel enjoy teaching others punch needle through workshops and event demonstrations, and they are part of an encouraging craft community on social media as well.

In this book the sisters help you explore this relaxing craft and teach you how to punch-needle through illustrations, photographs, and step-by-step instructions. You will learn the techniques, which punch needle tools to combine with which yarns, and information on sourcing materials. They have created contemporary punch needle projects for you to make, such as cushions, wall hangings, and practical accessories. You will also explore different ways to upcycle different materials.

You will start by creating small projects and move on to larger projects, allowing lots of scope for you to challenge yourself as you progress.

Their online store, The Modern Crafter, offers punch needle and embroidery kits and supplies. Using Siobhan's design experience and Rachel's needlework skills, they have built a successful business by creating modern, stylish punch needle and embroidery kits that everyone can enjoy.

HOW TO USE THIS BOOK

Throughout the book we have indicated which projects are best to start with first if you are a complete beginner.

Projects with one punch needle symbol are suitable for beginners, whereas those with two or three punch needle symbols will require the use of a sewing machine and sewing skills. Furthermore, it is often the finishing technique that is the hardest part, so we have categorized the projects on the basis of the technical ability of the required finish as well.

Level 1 –

Level 2 –

Level 3 –

Each project has its own punch needle stitch illustration showing where we punched a loop or flat stitch; these are shown by the boxes opposite. You can mark your design with an F for flat, or an L for loop, if you like a reminder.

Loop stitch

Flat stitch

We have provided access to the digital file templates. Find and download the templates at www.schifferbooks.com/punchtemplates.

We hope you will have fun making these projects and they inspire you to go on to create many more of your own projects. We absolutely love seeing your projects, so if you are on social media, share your makes with us *@the_modern_crafter*

Happy punching!

Rachel and Siobhan xx

TOOLS AND MATERIALS

Tools and Materials

PUNCH NEEDLE TOOLS

All punch needle tools work by creating a continuous loop as the needle is punched into the cloth. When you punch the tool in the cloth, it creates a loop: it is the loop that grips into the weave of the cloth. When the yarn is punched in rows like brickwork, the yarn will hold in place without the need for knots or glue.

The loop side is the traditional "up" side in rug making; however, in our projects we often like to combine the loop stitches and flat stitches on the same side by working on the front and the back of the frame. This technique creates a 3-D texture that we love, and we will teach you more on this under the "Punch Needle Techniques" section.

Punch needle tools come in different sizes: some for working with super-chunky yarn, others for working with finer yarn such as tapestry yarn, and even some with finer needle heads that are used for embroidery thread.

With a punch needle that works with super-chunky yarn, you can create bolder designs and bigger projects such as the Small Rug on page 103.

With a punch needle that works with finer yarn or embroidery threads, you can create more-detailed designs such as the Mini Patches (page 53) or Square Abstract Cushion (page 97).

In addition to matching the correct weight of yarn to your punch needle tool, you also need to match the correct weave of fabric with your punch needle tool, and we will talk about this further under the "Yarn" and "Fabric" sections on the next pages.

We have worked with two different punch needles in this book; namely, the size 10 regular Amy Oxford Punch Needle and the Lavor punch needle embroidery tool.

The **Lavor** punch needle embroidery tool is made from recycled plastic and comes with a threader and three needle heads. You can work between tapestry and aran weight yarns, as well as with embroidery threads. When setting the needle head into the handle, follow our instructions on the height to set your needle (see page 24). As a rule, the higher the needle height, the bigger the loop height, and the lower the needle height, the smaller the loop height.

The **Oxford** punch needle tool is made by punch needle artisan Amy Oxford, based in Vermont, USA. With extensive experience making rugs and teaching punch needle, Amy designed this punch needle tool. The Oxford punch needle tools are of exceptional quality and are comfortable to hold; the yarn threads straight onto the needle without the need of a threader, which makes changing yarn colors much easier. This tool is made to last a lifetime, and we recommend buying once and buying high quality that you won't need to throw away. The size 10 regular needle is our go-to favorite for most of our projects; this punches a quarter-inch loop size.

We have tried and tested many different tools, and we recommend investing in top-quality tools to give you the best experience of punch needle craft.

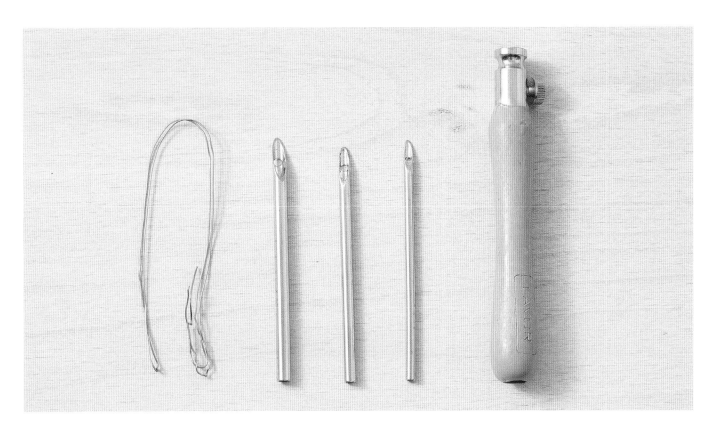

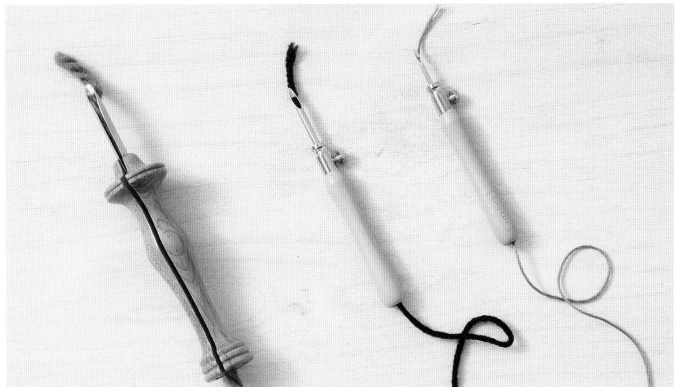

FABRIC

Punch needle fabric can be referred to as base or foundation cloth. The cloth that we worked with to create the projects in this book is linen, both natural and colored. Linen is less prone to fraying than cotton, and we love the texture and how the needles work with this natural cloth. The flax plant, which is used to make linen, has a lower impact on the environment, and undyed linen is 100 percent biodegradable.

As already mentioned, it is important to pair the size of the punch needle tool with your punch needle cloth. For example, the larger needles such as the Oxford size 10 will require an open-weave linen with approximately fifteen holes per inch. The Lavor punch needle embroidery tool requires a closer-weave linen, so aim for one with approximately twenty holes per inch—which will work with all three needle heads.

The reason for this is that the weave of the fabric grips the loop in place after the needle is punched into the cloth. If you have too big a weave for the smaller needle, the loop can't grip into the cloth. Have too fine a weave for the bigger needle and you will not even be able to punch it into the cloth!

We have outlined which cloth we used under each project. If you prefer, you can also use monk's cloth, which is a soft cotton cloth. In that case, look for a cloth with twelve holes per inch. If you do choose to work with monk's cloth, we recommend you secure your edges first by either taping the edges (using masking tape) or sewing the edges with zigzag or straight stitch on your sewing machine.

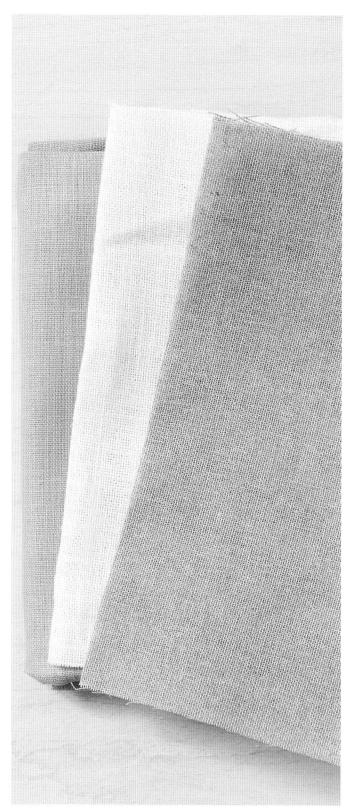

YARN

As mentioned in the introduction, punch needle is a great way to use up your yarn stash! If your yarn glides freely through the needle, you can punch with it.

You can achieve interesting textures through using a combination of different weights and types of yarns on the same project. With the size 10 Oxford needle, you can also double up finer yarn such as DK or aran weights. With the Lavor punch needle embroidery tool, we find that tapestry or aran yarns work well, in addition to six skeins of embroidery thread for the finer needle head.

Experiment with the patterns by using your preferred color pallet to make them unique to you.

For the Oxford size 10 regular needle, we find that super-chunky yarns work best. For those projects that will take more wear, such as the Small Rug, we recommend rug yarn or super-chunky coarse yarn specifically made for punch needle.

At the time of writing this book, we are at the start of our journey to develop a range of super-chunky British wool created specifically for punch needle. We have used the bronze color from our new range of wool in the projects within this book. If you would like to find out more about our 100 percent British wool for punch needle, please see our website at *www.themoderncrafter.co.uk*.

We encourage you to experiment with different fibers, but please use those that are kind to the environment. Some synthetic yarns include plastic, so we encourage you to research the yarn contents before you buy, to reduce the impact on the environment.

Here are examples of a combination of different weights of wools together, roving, punch needle yarn, and tapestry yarn. As you can see, they give very different results.

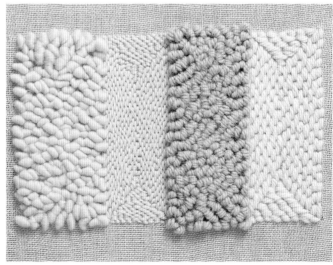

FRAMES

The punch needle technique requires the needle to be punched into the fabric; therefore the frame needs to be good enough to withhold this repetitive movement while keeping the fabric consistently drum taut.

If you use the wrong frame, you'll find that as you punch, the fabric will either slip out altogether or sag.

The Oxford size 10 needle requires a more robust frame such as canvas stretcher bars or a gripper hoop with a clamp screw to manage the size of the needle and thickness of wool, whereas the finer Lavor punch needle embroidery tool can also be used with a regular embroidery hoop.

CANVAS STRETCHER BAR FRAMES

Canvas stretcher bars come in pairs and in various sizes; they are traditionally used by artists for stretching canvas. They slot together so you can mix and match sizes to make square or rectangle shapes. This makes them a practical solution for cutting down on fabric waste, depending on the size of your project and the working area you need. You can also reuse them again and again!

For most of our projects, we have used two pairs of 18 in. frames slotted together to make a square frame. You will find a note, under each project, on the size of frame that we have used. Remember that you cannot punch into the fabric that covers the frame itself, so you need to make sure your project stays within the working area.

GRIPPER HOOPS

Gripper hoops come with a clamp screw and a thicker rim so that they grip the fabric taut while you punch into the cloth. They are great to work with; however, they are a little more restrictive on the size and shape of your projects. We recommend wooden gripper hoops over plastic hoops every time.

EMBROIDERY HOOP

This is a great option for smaller projects, since it takes less of a "punch" when working with the finer punch needle tool; you can punch straight on an embroidery hoop.

Essential Extras

1. Backing Cloths
We outline which backing cloths to use in each project.

2. Bag Handles and Poppers
These are essential for the bag projects.

3. Blank Paper
We used blank paper to cut out the abstract shapes to transfer some of the designs to the fabric.

4. Clover Clips
Useful for clipping back the fabric when whipping edges

5. Dowel Rod
Easily cut to size. Used in hanging baskets.

6. Fray Check
To avoid your project fraying once removed from the frame, apply Fray Check to the edges with a thin line.

7. HeatnBond Ultra Hold Adhesive
For creating the Patches project and attaching them to your clothing or bag

8. Magnetic Fastenings
Strong and easy to fit. Ideal for the Cross-Body Bag.

9. Marker or Erasable Pen
Draw around shapes or draw the design directly onto the fabric by using either a marker or erasable pen. For the projects that are entirely filled in with wool, the pen mark will be hidden; for projects where fabric is left exposed, use a water-erasable embroidery pen.

10 Punch Needle Tools
Our favorites: the Oxford size 10 and the Lavor punch needle embroidery tool

11. Rope handles
Used for the wall storage baskets

12. Roundheaded Pins
Handy for pinning the backing cloth in place before sewing or for pinning back a hem on a rug

13. Ruler
Use to outline the design for a crisp, straight line

14. Scissors and Snips
You will need a good pair of fabric scissors and yarn snips.

15. Seam Ripper
A handy tool for unpicking stitches without damage

16. Staple Gun
A quick and easy way to secure your fabric to the frame

17. Staple Remover
To remove the staples from your stretcher bar frame

18. Tape Measure
Handy for measuring seam allowance

19. Thread
Sewing thread is needed for finishing some of the projects.

20. Yarn
To provide texture and color

21. Yarn, Darning, and Embroidery Needles
Yarn needles are for whipping wool, darning needles for whipping hems, and embroidery needles for stitching fabrics together.

You May Also Need:
Sewing Machine and an Iron
Not essential for everything, but they will play a role in some of the projects.

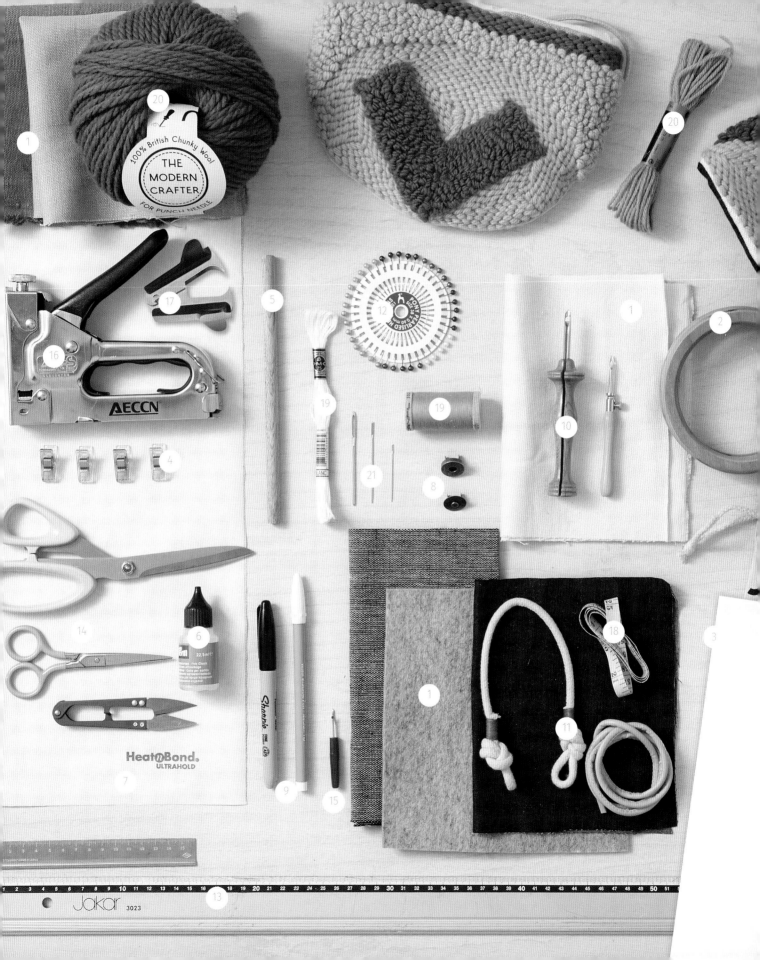

PREPARATION

Preparation

HOW TO STRETCH THE FABRIC

ON THE STRETCHER BAR FRAME

First, prepare your stretcher bar frame. Slot your frame together, making sure each side is straight and secure. You can staple-gun over the joins if you find it's loose.

1. Lay your fabric on a flat surface and place the frame on top. Cut the fabric to size, leaving a seam allowance of around 2.5 in.

2. Starting at the middle of one side of the frame, fold the fabric over once, and then again onto the frame.

3. Using the staple gun, secure the fabric in place.

4. Working on the opposite side, pull the fabric as taut in the middle as possible and secure it with the staple gun. Keep stretching and pulling the remainder of that side and staple-gun the fabric in place as you go.

5. Repeat the same process on the remaining two sides, making sure that the fabric is drum taut.

6. Trim the corners diagonally.

7. Fold and staple-gun your corners in place securely.

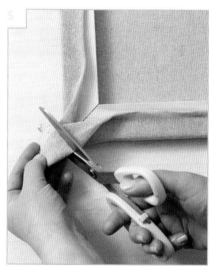

ON THE GRIPPER HOOP

1. Loosen the clamp screw on the top of your hoop.

2. Separate the top and bottom hoops and lay your fabric over the bottom hoop as smoothly as possible. Place the top hoop over the fabric and lightly tighten up the clamp.

3. Turn the hoop over to the back and pull the fabric up to stretch it across the frame.

4. Fully tighten the clasp back up, making sure the fabric is drum taut and there are no creases.

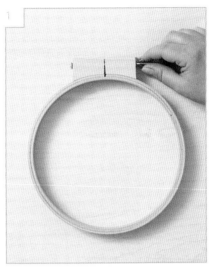

How to Thread the Needle

Oxford Punch Needle

1. Thread the yarn through the eye of the needle.

2. Push the yarn into the slot at the bottom of the handle.

3. Pull the yarn from the eye of the needle up until the yarn sits flush in the slot.

4. Pull the yarn back, leaving an inch of tail through the eye of the needle.

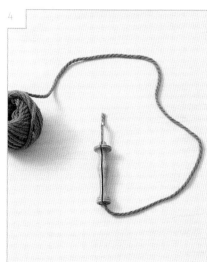

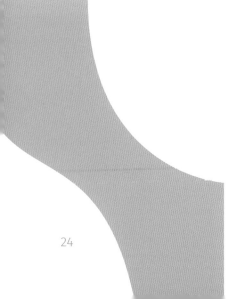

LAVOR PUNCH NEEDLE EMBROIDERY TOOL

1. Insert the chosen size of needle head into the handle of the punch needle. Set the needle head so you have about 0.25 in. showing. Use the screw on the right-hand side of the needle to tighten it in place. Make sure it is as tight as possible so that the needle will not slip when in use.

2. Straighten out your threader and thread the loop side through the eye of the needle. Fold the two ends of the threader over, securing in place.

3. Create a loop at the bottom of the threader and pick up the yarn; secure the yarn in place by tweezing the threader together. Pull the threader up through the needle.

4. Release the threader, then thread it through the back of the eye of the needle to the front. Pick up the yarn again and pull through.

5. Pull the yarn back down on the needle to leave 1 in. of yarn tail through the eye of the needle.

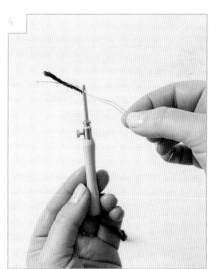

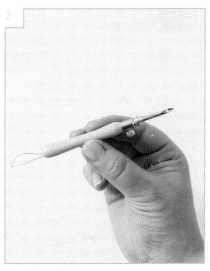

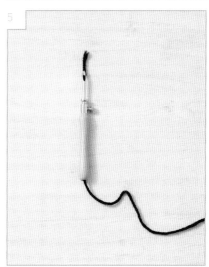

How to Transfer the Design

For every step-by-step project, we have provided an illustrated design with a note of how to transfer the scheme. The following are a few different ways to transfer the design:

~ Using a photocopier, scale up the design to the measurements given.

~ Cut out the design shapes from ordinary paper and outline them on the fabric with a marker pen.

~ Draw the design freehand onto paper and secure it to the back of your stretched fabric. Hold it against a light source and draw it on.

~ Draw the design freehand straight onto the fabric, using a strong light source behind to show the lines. Some of the shapes are simple enough to do this, and they will be unique to you since they will be drawn by your own hand too!

Find and download the templates here: www.schifferbooks.com/punchtemplates.

To enlarge the patterns in this book: The percentage shown beneath the templates at the back of the book will give the project size indicated. If you want to make the template larger or smaller, divide the size you want by the size you have, and turn it into a percentage. For example, if the size you want is 6 in. and the length of the pattern is 5 in., 6/5 = 1.20; 1.20 x 100 = 120%.This means you must print out your pattern at 120% (or program the photocopy machine to produce a copy that is 120% the size of the original).Remember, however, that if you make the size larger than the suggestion, you will need more materials.

PUNCH NEEDLE TECHNIQUES

As mentioned in the introduction, the loop side is the traditional side for punch needle work; however, we like to combine the loop and flat stitches together. To achieve this effect, you will need to work on both sides of your frame (1).

When you punch on the front of the frame, you will punch flat stitches, and by turning your frame over and following the same technique on the back of your frame, you will create the loop stitches on the display side.

Aim to stagger your stitches from one row to the next like brickwork, with the stitches and rows touching one another side by side. This will help close the gaps between stitches, keep the stitches secure together, and get a nice fuller look to your project. Don't worry about getting this perfect all the time—just most of the time (2).

We highly recommend that you outline the area that you are punching first before filling it in. By doing this you will achieve a neater finish.

The technique for all punch needle tools is the same; however, the stitch length will vary depending on the size of your punch needle tool.

For the Oxford size 10 punch needle, aim for six stitches per inch for the outer two rows, then four stitches per inch for filling in.

For the Lavor punch needle embroidery tool and tapestry yarn, aim for seven stitches per inch for the outer two rows, then six stitches per inch for filling in. When working with embroidery threads, aim for fifteen stitches per inch.

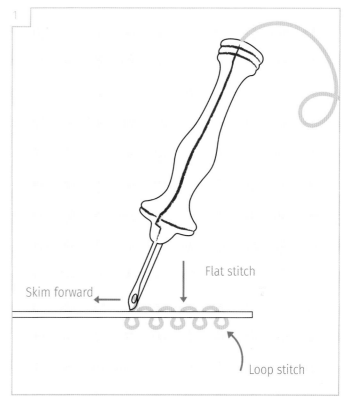

Skim forward

Flat stitch

Loop stitch

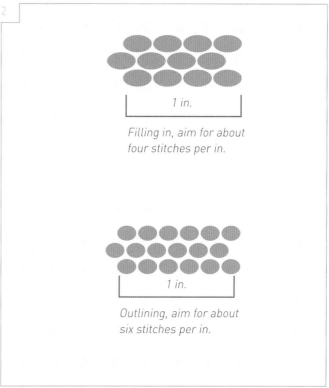

1 in.

Filling in, aim for about four stitches per in.

1 in.

Outlining, aim for about six stitches per in.

FLAT STITCHES

This is the technique for creating flat stitches. Note that you will be working on the front of your frame.

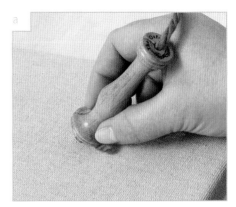

1. With your threaded needle, punch the tip of the needle into the fabric, with the top of the needle at a slight angle facing toward you (a).

2. Turn the frame over and pull the yarn tail through to the back, leaving approximately 1 in. of tail (b).

3. Turn the frame back over and lift your needle up gently just until you see the tip of the needle (c).

4. Glide your needle across the fabric and repunch, making sure that you punch down until the handle of your punch needle tool touches the fabric. It is important to do this on every punch to create a consistent loop length.

5. To turn your needle: turn the needle when it is down in the fabric, and then punch again with the tip of the needle in the direction to fill. Outline the section first, then fill in, working from the outer edge into the middle.

6. Try to stagger most of your stitches. To do this, aim for halfway down on your previous row and punch side by side so that the rows just touch one another. Don't worry if you don't manage this all the time, but try to achieve staggered stitches most of the time (d).

TIP: *Don't lift your needle up too high, since this will release your loop.*

TIP: *Make sure you have plenty of slack on your yarn so the yarn can move freely through the needle.*

TIP: *Punch close to your loop stitches by using your other hand to push the loop to the side.*

ENDING FLAT STITCHES

1. Turn your frame over to the back and create a slack loop on the yarn.

2. Snip in half, leaving a 1 in. yarn tail to snip away at the end.

LOOP STITCHES

The technique is the same as creating flat stitches, but you will be working on the back of your frame.

1. Turn the frame over to the back. With your threaded needle, punch the tip into the fabric, with the needle at an angle toward you.

2. Leave the yarn tail after your first punch and glide the needle across the fabric and repunch. By doing this you'll keep all the messy yarn tails at the back of your project, and you can tidy these up later.

29

ENDING LOOP STITCHES

1. On the back of the frame, use one hand to hold the base of the yarn and pull the needle up to create a bit of slack.

2. Snip the yarn, leaving 1 in. of yarn tail.

TIDYING YARN TAILS

Once you have finished your project, snip the yarn tails flush, so they are hidden and secure in between the stitches.

PROBLEM-SOLVING

MY YARN WON'T STAY IN

Make sure you have enough slack on your wool, by working with the ball of wool on the floor. Check also that there is not anything restricting the flow of the yarn through the needle—such as a knot that might be preventing the wool gliding through the needle. It is important to "skim" your needle over the fabric too; if you lift your needle up too high before making your next stitch, the loop will unravel. You can tighten your yarn back up by pulling it up through the top of the needle.

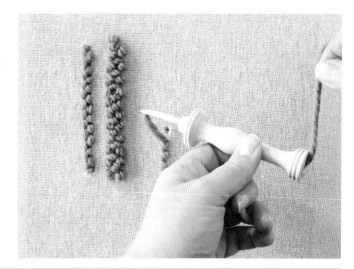

MY FLAT STITCHES LOOK LIKE LOOPS

When you punch into the fabric, make sure to punch the needle down until the handle of the punch needle touches the fabric. It's important to do this on every punch to achieve a consistent loop height.

Gently bring the needle up just until you see its tip, and then glide your needle across the fabric rather than lifting the needle. Not only could lifting the needle up release your yarn, it could also create a loop on the front. The flat stitches should be as flat as possible, while the loop stitches are a consistent size.

I'VE FINISHED MY PROJECT, BUT SOME YARN HAS COME LOOSE

Using your unthreaded needle, prod the yarn back through the fabric to neaten it up again.

Finishing Techniques

This section teaches you how to finish your project by using different hand-sewing techniques or with a sewing machine.

HEMMING

Hemming is a technique for neatly finishing the seams. We used this technique to finish our Small Rug project, for example:

1. Trim the corners diagonally and fold the corner over the first (1).

   Then fold each side of the corner. Pin in place (1a).

2. Double-fold the seam over on the underside of the rug. Using an iron and damp cloth, iron the seam to create a crisply folded hem.

3. Pin the folded hem in place as far back as you can, so that the edge of the fabric is not visible.

4. Thread your darning needle and tie a double knot at the end. Pick up a bit of the underside of your fabric and some yarn with the darning needle to secure the hem in place. Working up and over with the needle, whipstitch the hem in place. Aim for your stitches to be approximately 0.5 in. apart.

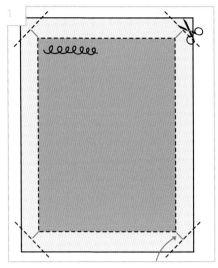

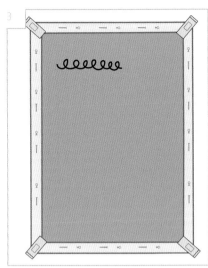

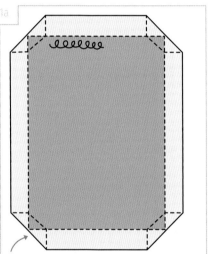

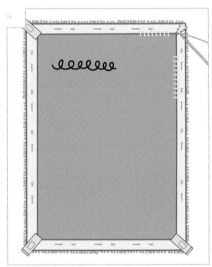

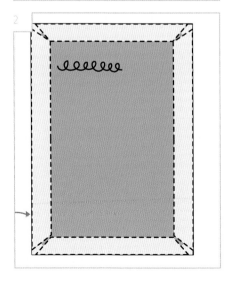

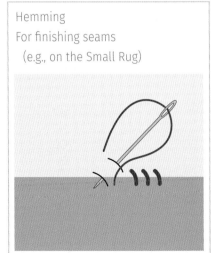

Hemming
For finishing seams
 (e.g., on the Small Rug)

WHIPSTITCH

This is a great way to get a nice decorative finish to your edges. Use whipstitch to cover up the edge of visible fabric. We regularly use it to finish wall hangings and have used it to finish the Hanging Plant Pot (see page 83), Trivet (see page 49), and Wall Storage Baskets (see page 75).

1. Cut an arm's length of yarn in your chosen color and thread the needle. Work on a flat surface and, from the back of your project to the front, insert the needle.

2. Lay off an inch of yarn tail along the edge to whip over to secure the yarn in place. This is much neater than making a knot to secure it.

3. Whip the needle up and over to create the whipstitches.

4. To secure the yarn, thread it back through under about an inch of previous whipstitches and pull the needle out. Snip the secured yarn away so that it is hidden. Keep going until you have whipped all the way around the edges.

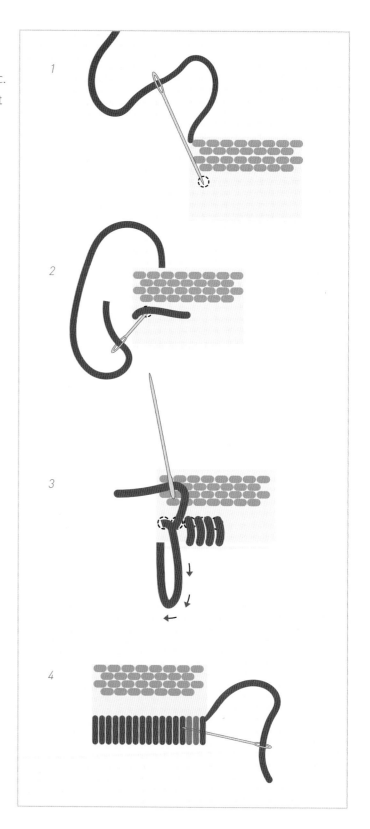

LADDER STITCH

Ladder stitch is a really useful stitch for closing gaps because you won't see the stitches when you've finished. Use this technique to finish projects such as toys and cushions.

1. Thread the embroidery needle with a light-colored thread and knot it at the end.

2. Insert the needle from the inside so that the knot is hidden out of sight.

3. Sew the needle through the seam of the opposite side of the fabric.

4. Repeat this move, working from one side to the other in the shape of a ladder.

5. Gently pull the thread tight and it will secure and hide the thread in place.

6. Fix in place by either tying a knot or looping your thread around the needle to create a secured knot.

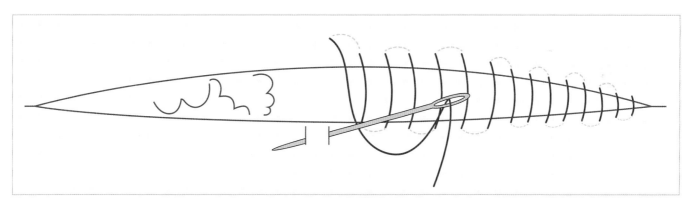

BACKSTITCH

We used backstitch when securing two pieces of fabric together for the Mushroom Toy, Turtle Toy, and Round Sunset Cushion. The stitches should touch one another.

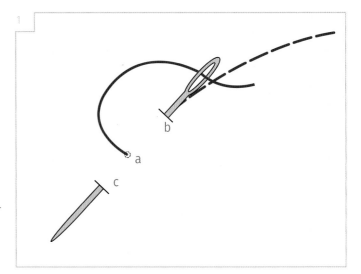

1. Thread your embroidery needle with a light-colored thread and knot it at the end.

2. Working as close to the edge of the yarn as possible —but making sure not to catch any of the yarn in your thread—sew the two pieces of cloth together

3. Insert the needle into the fabric and through to the other piece of fabric.

4. Working from right to left, bring the needle back up from the back of the fabric, one stitch length from your starting point (a–b).

5. Begin the next stitch by inserting the needle at your starting point and back up two stitch lengths away (c).

6. Continue keeping all the stitches the same length.

TACKING OR BASTING STITCH

The even-length basting stitch is very similar to the running stitch, but the stitches are longer. Simply weave the needle in and out of your fabric at regularly spaced intervals of about 0.25 in.

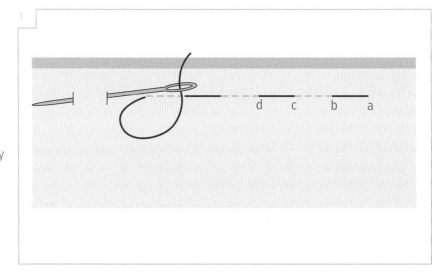

IRON PRESS

We really recommend using a cloth and iron to press over your finished creations once you remove them from the frame. This gives a nicer finish and helps with defining the fabric areas when preparing for your finishing stitches. Use the heat setting for the yarn you've used, so the wool setting for wool, for instance.

SEWING MACHINE

If you choose to finish some projects by using a sewing machine, attach a zipper foot, which will help your stitching get closer to the yarn edge, but be very careful not to sew on top of the yarn.

PROJECTS

Large Wall Hanging

Create a bold-textured focal point on your wall with this large wall hanging. This is a perfect project to use up a yarn stash! It is worked on the back and front of the frame to display flat and loop stitches together. This project was worked with roving yarn and super-chunky yarn to create lots of stunning textures.

TOOLS AND MATERIALS

Frame—
1 pair of 36 in. and 1 pair of 16 in. canvas stretcher bar frames to make a rectangular frame

Punch needle fabric—
Open-weave natural-colored linen

Punch needle tool—
Size 10 regular Oxford punch needle

Yarn—
500 g (approximately) of mixed roving + super-chunky yarn

Essential Extras
1 sheet letter paper
Iron + towel
Marker pen
Scissors
Staple gun
Staple remover
Wooden dowel
Yarn needle
Yarn snips

1. Assemble the stretcher bar frame. Then stretch and staple-gun the fabric to your frame. See the "Preparation" section on page 22.

2. The templates for this design can be found on page 122. You can scale this up by using the instructions supplied. Transfer the templates to paper and cut out the shapes.

   Using a ruler, draw the outer rectangle shape onto your fabric, then draw a straight line to divide the four sections of the pattern. Place your shapes onto the fabric and trace around them, using a marker pen. You can either follow the template or create your own design if you prefer.

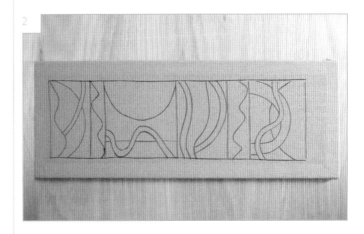

3. Outline the design on the back of the fabric as well. Decide which sections to punch in loop or flat stitches: it's a good idea to mark your sections with F for flat and L for loop as a reminder!

4. Follow the "Punch Needle Techniques" section on pages 27–30. Snip away yarn tails as you work, to tidy up your creation, and remove them from the frame.

5. Using fabric scissors, cut away the excess fabric, leaving a 1 in. seam allowance. Trim the corners diagonally to reduce the excess fabric when whipping the corners, but making sure to leave at least 0.5 in. of fabric.

6. Press your creation with an iron and towel.

7. Thread your yarn needle with about an arm's length of yarn and follow the "Whipstitch" section on page 34 (7a).

Once you've whipped around every edge, find a flat surface to work on. Lay your cut piece of dowel just above the top of the wall hanging. Attach it by whipping around the dowel, using your yarn needle. For this it's best to use rug yarn rather than roving yarn, since it's more robust and can take the weight for hanging (7b).

Cut half an arm's length of yarn and secure it to both ends of the dowel and hang it up, then step back to admire it!

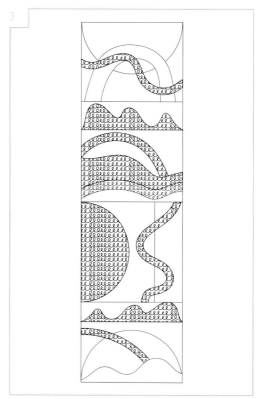

Hexagon Cushion

This Hexagon Cushion is fun to create and makes a cozy back support for your chair or sofa. It is quick and easy to make, so why not create a few in different contrasting colors to brighten up an area of your home.

TOOLS AND MATERIALS

Backing cloth—
Amber-colored linen

Frame—
2 pairs of 18 in. canvas stretcher bars to make a square frame

Punch needle fabric—
Open-weave white linen

Punch needle tool—
Size 10 regular Oxford punch needle

Yarn—
180 g (approximately) of super-chunky yarn or rug yarn

Essential Extras
Fiberfill
Marker pen
Needle + thread
Pins
Scissors
Staple gun
Staple remover
Yarn snips

1. Assemble your stretcher bar frame. Stretch and staple-gun the fabric to your frame.

2. Transfer your template from page 121. You can scale this up by using the instructions supplied.

   Having attached your template to the back of the frame, hold it up to a light source and use a marker pen to draw the design onto your fabric. Alternatively, cut one triangle shape to size and, using a ruler, outline it six times to create the hexagon shape.

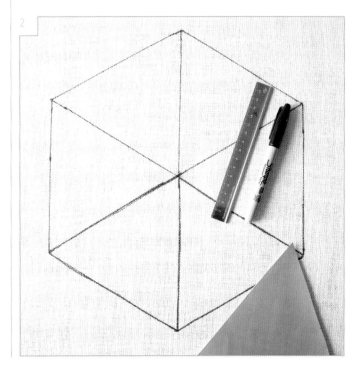

3. Decide which areas you will punch in flat stitches and which in loop stitches. Here we decided to punch this design entirely on the back of the frame, to display loop stitches on the final cushion.

   Follow the "Punch Needle Techniques" section on pages 27–30. Snip away yarn tails to tidy up your creation, and remove them from the frame.

4. Using fabric scissors, cut away the excess fabric, leaving a 1 in. seam allowance.

5. Lay your finished creation on top of the backing cloth and cut around the hexagon to create an identically shaped backing cloth.

6. Pin the right sides of your hexagon and backing cloth together, leaving the bottom unpinned to remind you not to sew this section.

7. Using a zipper foot or backstitch, sew around the hexagon, getting as close as you can to the punch needle stitches without sewing over the stitches. If you prefer to hand-sew with backstitch, follow the "Finishing Techniques" instructions on page 36.

8. Turn to the right side and stuff with fiberfill. Close the gap with ladder stitch, following the "Finishing Techniques" instructions on page 35.

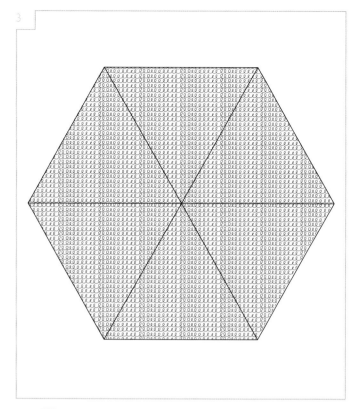

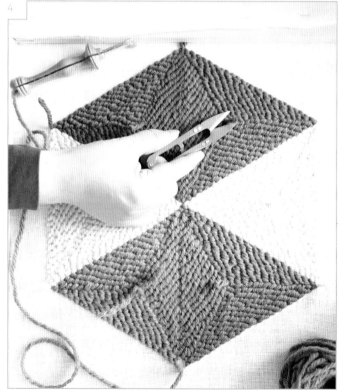

Trivet

Our stylish trivet will protect wooden surfaces from getting damaged from hot pots or cups. This modern design also makes the perfect centerpiece for any home. It's simple and quick to make and can be made in colors to match your décor.

TOOLS AND MATERIALS

Frame—
2 pairs of 12 in. canvas stretcher bars to make a square frame

Punch needle fabric—
Open-weave white linen

Punch needle tool—
Size 10 regular Oxford punch needle

Yarn—
150 g (approximately) of super-chunky yarn; we used British punch needle wool and super-chunky yarn

Essential Extras

Marker pen
Ruler
Scissors
Staple gun
Staple remover
Yarn needle
Yarn snips

1. Assemble the stretcher bar frame. Stretch and staple-gun the fabric to your frame.

2. The templates are on page 127. Since this is a simple design, you can easily transfer the design freehand.

   Using a ruler, mark the middle point on the fabric and draw a straight line down the middle. We used a glass to draw around for the circle; the other shapes were then drawn freehand.

3. We highly recommend that you punch this design entirely on one side of the frame; that way you can then use your finished project on either side, since it will sit evenly on the surface. Follow the "Punch Needle Techniques" section on pages 27–30. Snip away yarn tails to tidy up your creation, remove from the frame, and press the trivet, using a towel and iron on gentle heat.

4. Using fabric scissors, cut away the excess fabric, leaving a 1 in. seam allowance.

5. Trim the corners diagonally and lay your finished creation on a flat surface.

6. Using an arm's length of yarn at a time and your yarn needle, whipstitch around the edge until complete (6a).

   Start by securing 1 in. of yarn along the seam (6b).

   To secure the yarn at the end of your row, thread the yarn back through around 0.5 in. of previous stitches (6c).

   You can read our further guidance for whipstitch on page 34.

   Your trivet is now ready to use.

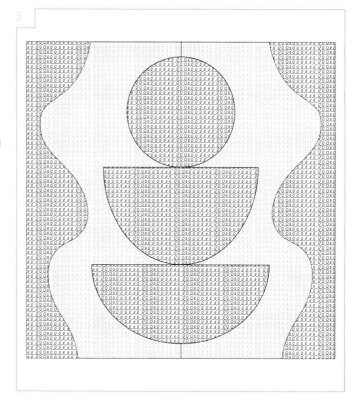

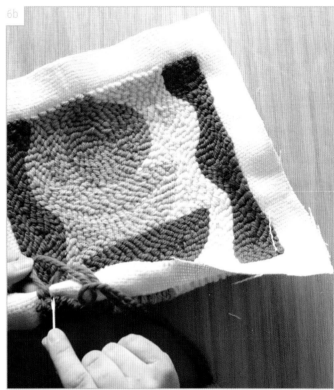

Mini Patches

Upcycle bags or clothing with these fun and colorful Mini Patches—they can go on almost anything! Make a number of them at the same time and use embroidery thread and the finer punch needle embroidery tool to really enjoy creating these eye-catching patches, which everyone from kids to adults will love.

TOOLS AND MATERIALS

Bags—
Canvas bag

Frame—
8 in. gripper hoop

Punch needle fabric—
Close-weave linen or organic cotton

Punch needle tool—
Lavor punch needle embroidery tool with finest needle tip

Yarn—
2 skeins (roughly) of embroidery thread per patch of the colors you want to use

Essential Extras
Embroidery needle
Fray Check (or similar)
HeatnBond ultra-hold iron-on adhesive (or similar)
Marker or embroidery pen
Scissors
Yarn snips

1. Stretch the fabric onto your gripper hoop, following the directions on page 23.

2. The templates for this project are on page 125. Transfer the designs onto paper, then cut out and secure to the back of your fabric. Using a water-erasable marker pen, trace your designs onto the cloth. It's helpful to mark where each color should go as a rough guide.

3. Thread your needle and follow the "Punch Needle Techniques" on pages 27–30. Outline each shape first by punching on the front of the frame before turning the frame over to follow the outline as a guide while filling in the rest of the patch. Our patch was punched to show loops only. When working with embroidery thread, it's important to stagger the stitches, since the gaps are not quite as forgiving as when working with a chunky rug yarn.

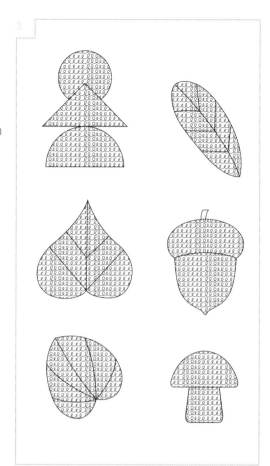

4. Once you have finished punch-needling the patches, remove them from the frame and cut around each one. Cut a piece of HeatnBond (or similar adhesive fabric) to fit this area.

5. Preheat your iron to medium heat, no steam. Place the adhesive side onto the back of your punch needle patch. Press and hold on the paper liner for two seconds; repeat until the entire surface is thoroughly bonded.

6. Leave to cool before peeling off the paper; otherwise all of your glue will come off and the patch won't stick.

7. Now that the underside of your patch is covered with adhesive and has been left to cool completely, you are ready to cut around your patch. Trim, using very sharp scissors, and be careful to work close to the punch needle edge, but without cutting into any of the stitches. Add Fray Check (or similar product) to the patch edges to minimize the risk of fraying and to make sure the edges are very secure.

8. Peel off the paper backing, and you should be able to see that your patch has a clear layer of glue on it.

   Your patch is now ready to iron onto your chosen item—when ironing on, *place the wrong side down* against the fabric, cover with a tea towel, and iron on medium heat until bonded.

4

7

5

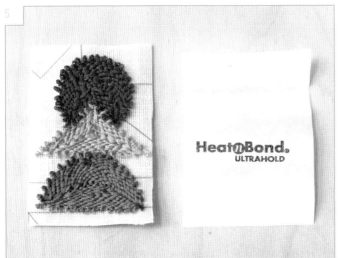

6

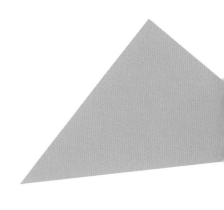

Mushroom Toy

This Mushroom Toy will make a beautiful gift for those little people in your life. Punched on both sides of the frame to bring the mushroom house to life, it lets everyone's imagination wonder about who lives inside this magical home!

TOOLS AND MATERIALS

Frame—
2 pairs of 18 in. canvas stretcher bars to make a square frame

Punch needle fabric—
Open-weave white linen + backing cloth—peach-colored linen

Punch needle tool—
Size 10 regular + Lavor punch needle embroidery tool

Yarn—
180 g (approximately) of super-chunky rug yarn + aran yarn for the windows

Essential Extras
Fiberfill
Fray Check (or similar)
Marker pen
Needle + thread
Roundheaded pins
Scissors
Staple gun
Staple remover
Yarn snips

1. Assemble your stretcher bar frame. Stretch and staple-gun the fabric to your frame.

2. Transfer the template from page 123. You can scale this up by using the instructions supplied. Copy the template, holding the frame up to the light and using your marker pen to draw the design onto your fabric, or draw the design freehand.

   Turn the frame over and redraw the outline on the back of your frame too, since you will be punching on both sides of the frame.

3. Decide in advance which sections you will punch in flat stitches and which you will punch to display loop stitches. If you like, mark these on the fabric, using an F for flat and L for loop as a reminder.

TIP: Use your opposite hand to move loops out of the way so as to get closer to the loop edges when punching flat stitches. We used aran-weight yarn and the biggest needle head with the Lavor punch needle embroidery tool for the windows.

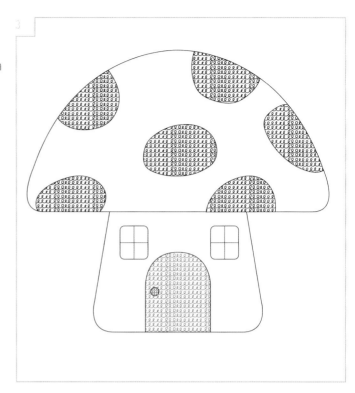

4. Follow the "Punch Needle Techniques" section on pages 27–30 (4a). Snip away yarn tails to tidy up your work, and remove it from the frame (4b).

5. With sharp fabric scissors, cut away the excess fabric, leaving a 1 in. seam allowance around the mushroom. Use a thin line of Fray Check on the outer edge to prevent fraying. Lay your finished creation on top of the backing cloth and cut around your mushroom to create an identical shape.

6. Pin the right sides of your mushroom and backing cloth together, leaving the bottom and both sides underneath the top of the mushroom unpinned (you'll sew these areas together after you turn back to the right side).

Using backstitch, sew around the mushroom, getting as close as you can to the punch needle stitches but being careful not to sew into the punched stitches. See our instructions for backstitch on page 36.

7. Clip small snips into the seam, around the top of the mushroom, before turning to the right side. This will make the edge smoother.

Use ladder stitch to sew the seams under the top of the mushroom on either side (see page 35 for instructions). You may need to snip into the corner of the fabric to get closer stitches to the yarn edge. If you do snip the fabric, be careful not to cut into any stitches.

Stuff the mushroom with fiberfill.

8. Fold the bottom seams to the inside and sew together to close the gap with invisible stitch. Before sewing your last few stitches, add more stuffing if necessary.

Mini Wall Hanging

This adorable wall hanging will make a beautiful gift or a focal point for a nursery wall. Create layers of texture by working with different types of yarn and a selection of colors to suit your décor. The tassels are easy to make, and they finish off the piece really nicely too.

TOOLS AND MATERIALS

Frame—
1 pair of 18 in.
+ 1 pair of 16 in. canvas stretcher bars to make a rectangular frame

Punch needle fabric—
Open-weave white linen

Punch needle tool
Size 10 regular Oxford punch needle

Yarn—
300 g (approximately) of super-chunky yarn—wool, rug yarn, and roving yarn

Essential Extras
Marker pen
Roundheaded pins
Ruler
Scissors
Staple gun
Staple remover
Yarn needle
Yarn snips

1. Assemble your stretcher bar frame. Stretch and staple-gun the fabric to your frame.

2. Transfer the template from page 122. Scale this up by using the instructions supplied. We drew the design freehand, using a ruler to mark the edges; alternatively you can secure the fabric to the back of the frame and, using a light source, trace the design onto your fabric.

3. Decide which sections to punch in flat stitches and which to punch in loop stitches. We punched all the rainbow in loop stitches, then used a variation between flat and loop stitches for the hills.

4. Follow the "Punch Needle Techniques" section on pages 27–30. Snip away yarn tails to tidy up your work, and remove it from the frame. Using fabric scissors, cut away the excess fabric, leaving a 1 in. seam allowance. Trim the corners diagonally.

5. To whip the edges, cut an arm's length of yarn, thread the needle, and whip with white yarn. For a smart finish, change the colors as you work to match the color of the hills at the bottom of the design.

   Press the wall hanging with a cloth and warm iron.

How to Make Tassels

1. Using a small book or piece of thick card, wrap your chosen yarn around from top to bottom about ten times. This depends on the thickness of your yarn and how long and thick you want the tassels. Cut a piece of yarn about 4 in. long and insert it through the underside of the yarn. Then pull this piece of yarn up to the top and tie a knot.

2. Remove the yarn from the book (or card).

3

5a

4

5b

3. Cut another piece of yarn about 4 in. long in a contrasting color. Make a loop with one end of the yarn, leaving about a 2 in. end visible. Continue to wrap the remainder of the yarn. You should now have a loop and two small ends of yarn.

4. Secure the end of the yarn by threading the wrapping end through the loop. Pull the other end up and it will hide the end, making it tight too. Snip the other end away so it is hidden, and secure as well.

5. Using a yarn needle, attach the tassel to the wall hanging, knotting it at the end. Repeat this process for as many tassels as you have (5a).

   Trim the bottom of all the tassels to the same length (5b).

6. Cut a piece of dowel to size.

7. Cut an arm's length of yarn and whip around the dowel to keep it secure. Select a more robust yarn than roving yarn, cut another length, and secure on both ends of the dowel to hang up your Mini Wall Hanging.

Turtle Toy

The super-cute turtle will bring a smile to every little one's face. Make it with coarser punch needle yarn so it is harder wearing, since this adorable toy is certain to get lots of cuddles!

TOOLS AND MATERIALS

Backing cloth—
Amber-colored linen

Frame—
2 pairs of 18 in. canvas
stretcher bars to make a
square frame

Punch needle fabric—
Open-weave white linen

Punch needle tool—
Size 10 regular Oxford
punch needle

Yarn—
200 g (approximately) of
super-chunky yarn (e.g., rug
yarn)

Essential Extras

Fiberfill
Fray Check (or similar)
Marker pen
Needle + thread
Roundheaded pins
Scissors
Staple gun
Staple remover
Yarn snips

1. Assemble your stretcher bar frame. Stretch and staple-gun the fabric to your frame.

2. Transfer the template from page 126. Scale this up by using the instructions supplied, or draw the design freehand. Use a ruler to outline the hexagons on the back for straight lines.

3. Decide which sections you will punch on the back and which you will punch on the front of the frame to display flat and loop stitches together. Mark these with an F for flat or L for loop if it helps you keep track of where you are.

4. Snip away yarn tails to tidy up your work, and remove them from the frame. Using sharp scissors, cut away the excess fabric, leaving a 1 in. seam allowance around the turtle. Use Fray Check (or similar product) around the edges of the fabric to prevent the seam from fraying (4a, 4b).

5. Lay your turtle on top of the backing cloth and cut around the shape to create an identical backing cloth.

6. Use an iron and towel to press the turtle flat (6a).

   Pin the right sides of your turtle and backing cloth together but leave the bottom section and under each of the top arms unpinned, since you will hand-sew these sections later (6b).

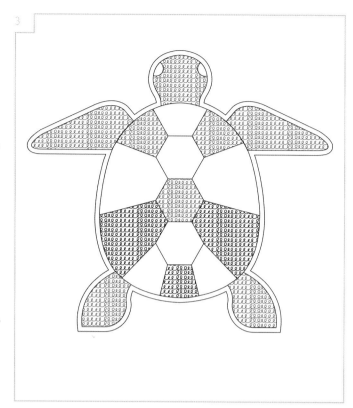

7. Using backstitch, hand-sew around the turtle, getting as close as you can to the punch needle stitches while being careful not to stitch over any of the yarn.

8. To get a smoother seam, create darts around the head by snipping into the seam allowance—be very careful not to remove your stitches.

9. Turn to the right side and hand-sew under the top arms, using ladder stitch. If you need to, you can cut into the fabric slightly around the corners at the arms to sew closer to the yarn. For the instructions on how to do ladder stitch, see the "Finishing Techniques" section on page 35.

10. Start to stuff the top of the turtle with fiberfill. You might need to trim around the bottom feet and snip into the corners of each side of the legs as well, so you can sew the gap closer to the edge of the yarn.

11. Finally, fold the front and back seams to the inside and sew together again with invisible stitch. Before fully sewing, add more stuffing if necessary. See page 35 for instructions on invisible stitch.

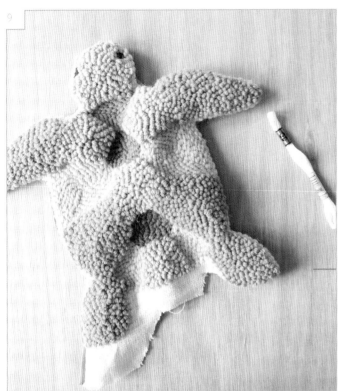

Wall Storage Baskets

These abstract, stylish, and useful wall storage baskets are handy stationery holders for any home office or hobby room. They are perfect for storing your favorite stationery or some of your project tools such as punch needle tools, rulers, pens, and scissors.

TOOLS AND MATERIALS

Backing cloth—
3 mm wool felt
+ 2 felt hanging strips, 20 mm wide × 90 mm high

Frame—
2 pairs of 18 in. canvas stretcher bars, making a square frame

Punch needle—
Size 10 regular Oxford punch needle

Punch needle fabric—
Open-weave white linen

Yarn—
500 g (approximately), e.g., rug yarn and super-chunky roving yarn

Essential Extras
1 sheet letter paper
5 mm natural cotton piping cord
Clover clips
Embroidery needle + thread
Iron + damp towel
Marker pen
Scissors
Staple gun
Staple remover
Waxed cotton thread (optional)
Wooden dowel
Yarn needle
Yarn snips

1. Assemble your stretcher bar frame. Stretch and staple-gun the fabric to your frame.

2. Using the templates on page 124, scale the pattern to size by using a light source, and trace the design onto the fabric.

3. Decide which sections you will punch on the back and which you will punch on the front of the frame to display flat and loop stitches together.

   Below are the designs we chose to work with.

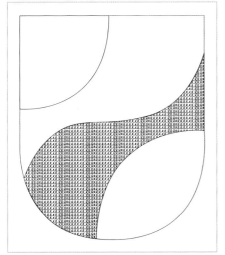
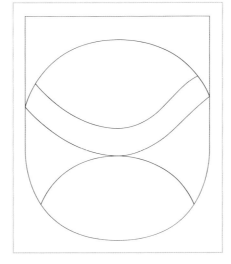

4. Follow the "Punch Needle Techniques" section on pages 27–30. Snip the yarn tails and remove from the frame. Press your design with a warm steam iron, covering it carefully with a damp tea towel. Don't be tempted to skip this step, since it really makes a huge difference to the quality of finish.

5. Trim down your design, leaving a 0.5 in. seam allowance around the edges. Add Fray Check (or similar product) to the cut edge of the fabric. This stops the fabric from fraying and means you won't worry about it while you're working.

6. Cut your backing fabric, remembering to leave a 0.5 in. seam allowance around the edges. If you are using felt (as we have here), you will want this top edge to line up flush with your front punch needle panel when it's sewn—so there is no need to add seam allowance to the top edge of your felt. We used felt for structure and also for ease of sewing, since the edge won't fray. At this point it's also a good idea to mark the location of the felt strips. Do this by marking the center along the top edge and measuring out on each side 2 in., and down from the top edge by 0.75 in. Mark a small dot.

7. Place the fabric right sides facing and pin or clip them together (we used clover wonder clips, which work well with thicker fabrics). Sew all around the edges—remembering to leave the top open. Leave a 0.5 in. seam allowance. Clip carefully into the curve of the pouch and then turn it so the right side is facing out. Press again.

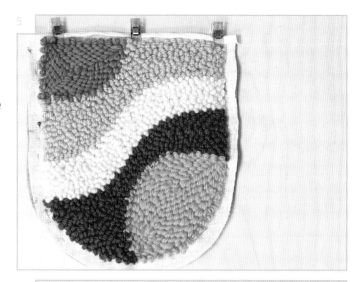

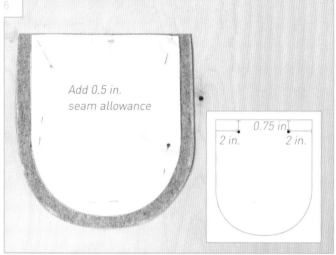

Add 0.5 in. seam allowance

0.75 in.

2 in.   2 in.

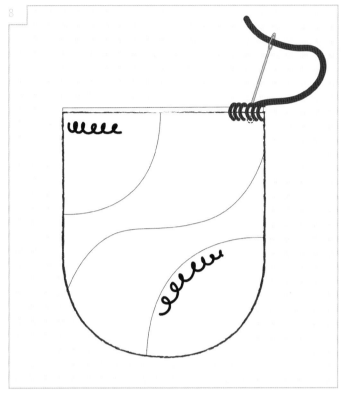

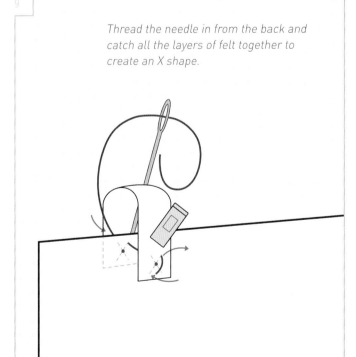

Thread the needle in from the back and catch all the layers of felt together to create an X shape.

8. Roll the top edge down and clip it in place. Begin whipstitching from one corner to the other.

9. Cut the felt straps for attaching to the back panel, and place on the dots as marked in step 6. Use clover clips to keep them in place. Thread the needle with embroidery thread and stitch an X to secure everything in place.

10. You're now ready to thread your dowel through the straps. Attach the rope by wrapping it around the dowel, and secure it with a knot. We finished by wrapping a waxed cotton cord around the end of the knot.

Tech Case

Create this beautiful and original Tech Case—in this example, for an iPad—using your own choice of yarn and colors. It is both a simple design and a practical project for you to create with your own hands. It will keep your precious tech snug and safe and look stylish as well!

TOOLS AND MATERIALS

Backing cloth—
Peach-colored linen + calico for lining

Frame—
1 pair of 18 in. × 1 pair of 12 in. canvas stretcher bar to make a rectangular frame

Punch needle fabric—
Open-weave white linen

Punch needle tool—
Size 10 regular Oxford punch needle

Yarn—
200 g (approximately) of super-chunky yarn (e.g., rug yarn)

Essential Extras
Marker pen
Needle + thread
Roundheaded pins
Ruler
Scissors
Sewing machine
Staple gun
Staple remover
Yarn snips

1. Assemble the stretcher bar frame. Stretch and staple-gun the fabric to your frame.

2. Since iPads vary in size, center it on the fabric and mark the corners. Remove the iPad and with a ruler draw straight lines to match up the corners to making a rectangle.

3. Use the template on page 121. Scale the pattern to size, then use a light source and trace the design onto your fabric.

4. Decide which sections you will punch on the back and which you will punch on the front of the frame to display flat and loop stitches together (4a).

   Turn the pattern to the front, snip away yarn tails to tidy up your work, and remove it from the frame (4b).

5. Using fabric scissors, cut away the excess fabric, leaving a 1 in. seam allowance all around.

6. Lay your finished creation on top of the backing cloth and cut around your iPad case to create an identically shaped backing cloth. Pin the right sides of the case and backing cloth together, leaving the top unpinned to remind you not to sew this section.

7. Create the lining in the same way, by sewing two pieces of lining cloth together. Leave the top unsewn.

8. Turn your iPad case and the lining right side out. Insert the lining into your iPad case. Fold the lining and the top seam of the case into the backing cloth and the front of the design. Press the seams by using an iron and cloth.

9. Check that the iPad will be nice and snug by inserting it. If there are any issues, you should be able to still adjust your lining width. Sew the lining to the front and back seams, using ladder stitch.

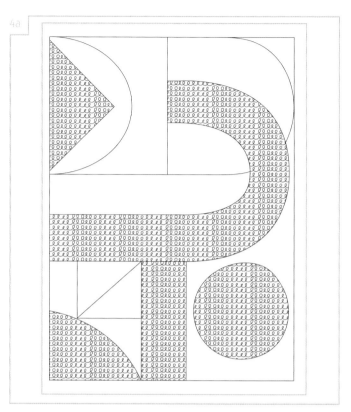
4a

4b

5

6

7

8

9

Hanging Plant Pot

Create this simple and elegant hanging plant pot to show off your houseplants. You can easily remove the plant to keep it watered, and move it around in your home to catch the sunlight. The pattern is easy to follow and easy to draw—all you need to think about is which wool colors to pick!

TOOLS AND MATERIALS

Backing cloth—
Peach-colored linen
+ calico for the lining

Frame—
1 pair of 22 in.
+ 1 pair of 12 in. canvas stretcher bars to make a rectangular frame

Punch needle fabric—
Open-weave white linen

Punch needle tool—
Size 10 regular Oxford punch needle

Yarn—
200 g (approximately) of super-chunky yarn (e.g., rug yarn and wool)

Essential Extras
Marker pen
Needle + thread
Roundheaded pins
Ruler
Scissors
Sewing machine with zipper foot
Staple gun
Staple remover
Yarn needle
Yarn snips

1. Using a sheet of letter paper, wrap it around your plant pot, marking the top, bottom, and joining sides of the pot. Use clear adhesive tape to join more than one sheet of paper together if you need to.

2. Lay the sheet flat. Using your marker lines and a ruler, draw out the rectangle shape. Add an extra 0.5 in. on to the length of each end for extra allowance, to make sure the pot will fit securely inside.

3. Cut out the sheet of letter paper to your marked size and draw the design onto it—by hand-drawing the design this way, you can also make it fit your plant pot. Otherwise, there is the option to scale the design to 19.5 × 6 in. and trace the design onto the fabric.

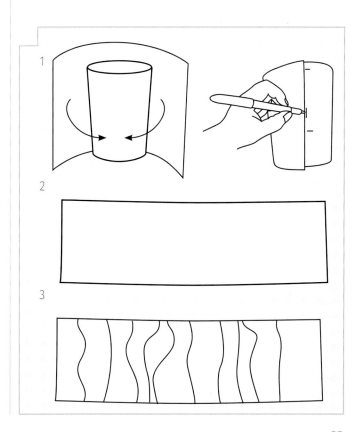

4. Assemble the stretcher bar frame. Stretch and staple-gun the fabric to your frame. Secure the paper with the design to the back of your fabric and, holding it up to a light source, draw the design onto the fabric. Use a ruler to get straight edges if you need to. Make sure you can also see the design on the back of the frame, since you will be punching on both sides.

5. Decide which sections you will punch in flat and loop stitches, and note it on the fabric if you want.

6. Follow the "Punch Needle Techniques" section on pages 27–30. Snip away yarn tails to tidy up your work (6a, 6b).

TIP: Before removing your finished project from the frame, double-check that the width will fit around your plant pot, by measuring its length against your sheet of paper. Add extra stitches if needed.

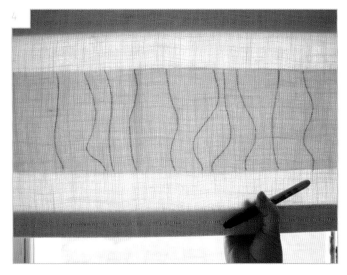

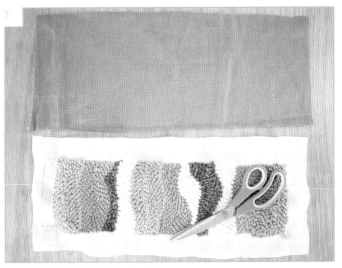

7. Remove the work from your frame and, using fabric scissors, cut away the excess fabric, leaving a 1 in. seam allowance around your punch needle fabric. Cut out an identical backing cloth by laying your project on the cloth and cutting around it.

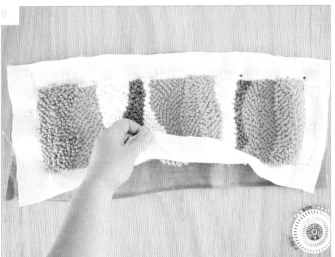

8. Pin the right sides of your hanging plant pot and backing cloth together, leaving the bottom unpinned to remind you not to sew this section.

9. Using a sewing machine with a zipper foot, sew the backing cloth and top and sides to the plant pot.

10. Trim the corners before turning to the right side so you get a neater-shaped corner.

11. For the base of the hanging plant pot, turn your plant pot upside down onto the cloth and draw around it (11a).

Draw up a second circle to create an extra-sturdy base (11b). That done, cut an extra seam allowance around the circles of 0.5 in. Whipstitch the two sides together, using the wool needle and some of your rug yarn. Cut a piece of yarn approximately the length of your arm and knot it at the end.

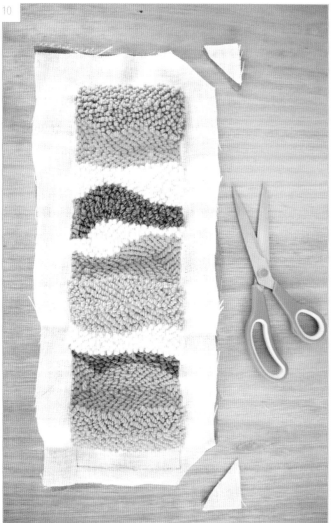

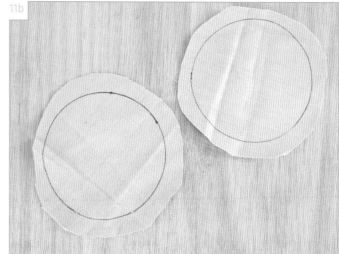

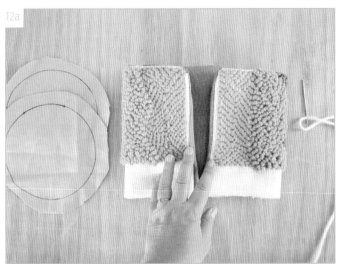

12. Fold your punch needle work in half (12a).

Insert the needle from the back of the cloth so that the knot is secure but hidden. Start to whipstitch the sides together, making sure not to pull too hard (12b).

Keep checking that your plant pot will still fit. If the yarn runs out, thread it through the seam to secure it (12c, 12d).

At the top, snip the yarn, leaving about 1 in. Tie a knot and tuck it behind the whipstitches to hide it (12e).

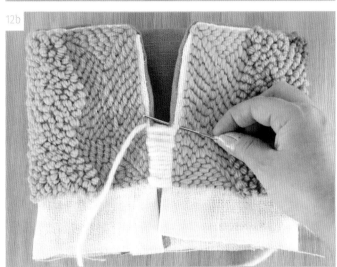

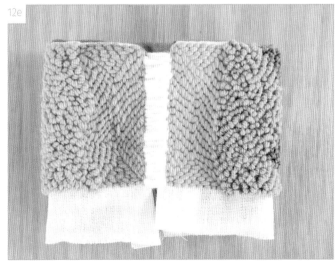

13. Next, with your punch needle project inside out, pin your base cloths to the outer cloths. You might find it easier to do this by turning the plant pot upside down and stretching and pulling down the project first.

14. Using thread and a needle, sew the base, using basting stitch (14a).

Take your time with this part, and you can separate each part of cloth first to make sure you are getting as close as you can to your punch needle stitches and that you are sewing through the base cloth, punch needle cloth, and lining cloth (14b).

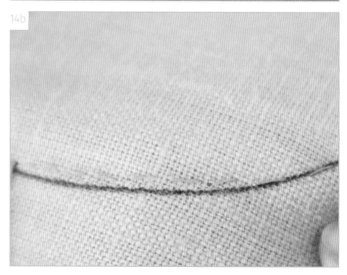

15. Once you have sewn the base, turn your piece to the right side. Whip the edge all the way around the top to hide the visible fabric. Follow the instructions in the "Whipstitch" section on page 34 (15a, 15b).

16. To create the hanger, cut an arm's length of yarn. Thread the needle and insert it into your project underneath the whipped stitches. Once through, remove the needle and double the yarn up. Repeat these another two times at your chosen insert points. We made a triangle shape, with two pieces of hanging yarn at the front sides and one at the back of the plant pot where the two ends join.

17. Tie all the yarn together in a knot and it is ready to hang.

Round Sunset Cushion

The Round Sunset Cushion can be easily carried from room to room by using its handle. It could be used as a floor cushion or, by using less stuffing, would also make a comfortable seat cushion pad for a hard chair.

TOOLS AND MATERIALS

Frame—
2 pairs of 18 in. canvas stretcher bar, making a square frame

Punch needle fabric—
Open-weave natural linen + backing fabric—amber-colored linen

Punch needle tool—
Size 10 regular Oxford punch needle

Yarn—
400 g (approximately) of super-chunky yarn (e.g., rug yarn)

Essential Extras

Fiberfill

Marker pen

Needle + thread

Roundheaded pins

Scissors

Sewing machine—optional

Staple gun

Staple remover

Yarn snips

1. Assemble your stretcher bar frame. Stretch and staple-gun the fabric to your frame.

2. Transfer the template from page 123. Scale this up by using the instructions supplied. If you are confident you can, always draw it out freehand. Make sure you can see the design outline on the back of your frame too.

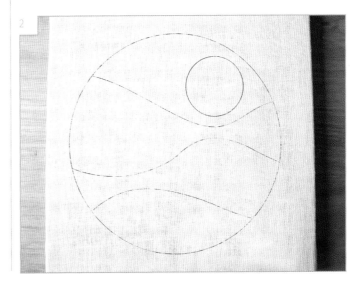

3. Decide which sections you would like in flat stitches and which in loop stitches. This project combines flat and loop stitches together by punching on both sides of the frame.

4. Follow the "Punch Needle Techniques" section on pages 27–30 (4a).

   Remove it from the frame and then snip away the yarn tails to tidy up your work (4b).

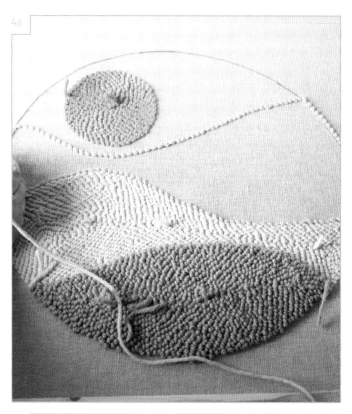

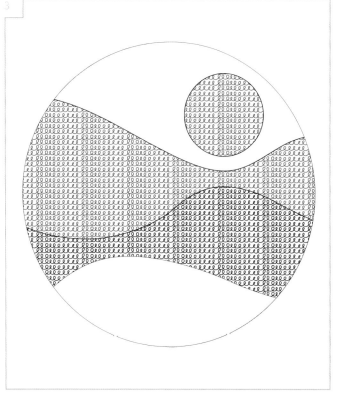

5. Using fabric scissors, cut away the excess fabric, leaving a 1 in. seam allowance. Lay the backing fabric on a flat surface, with the round cushion on top. Cut around the backing fabric to make it the same size.

6. To make the handle, measure two pieces of backing cloth and pin them together. Using a sewing machine, sew all sides of the handle together.

7. Pin the handle to the right side of the backing cloth at the top of the cushion.

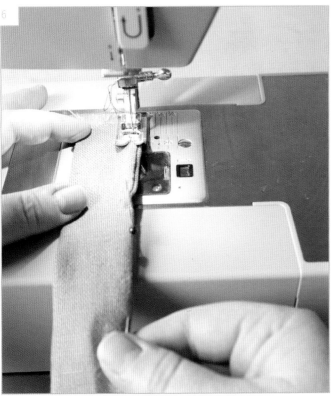

8. Lay your finished creation on top, with the right side facing inward. Pin both together, leaving a 5 in. gap at the bottom of the cushion so you can turn it back to the right side later.

9. Either using basting stitch or a sewing machine with zipper foot, sew as close as you can to the edge—being careful not to sew on top of the yarn.

10. Before turning it back to the right side, using small scissors, snip around the seam to create darts, which will help create the rounded shape. Be careful not to snip into your stitches.

11. Turn your cushion to right side out (11a).

Stuff it with a cushion pad or fiberfill. Sew up the gap with ladder stitch. Follow the "Ladder Stitch" section on page 35. For a set of cushions, keep the pattern similar and vary the yarn colors a little (11b).

Square Abstract Cushion

Some of our favorite things to create are cushions—and this abstract-design cushion will give a modern edge to any room. It's handmade with beautiful, top-quality linen and tapestry wool. However, we are sure your friends will be asking you which retail store you bought it from!

TOOLS AND MATERIALS

Backing fabric—
  Amber linen

Frame—
  2 pairs of 18 in. canvas stretcher bars to make a square frame

Punch needle fabric—
  Peach linen

Punch needle tool—
  Lavor punch needle embroidery tool, using the biggest size of needle head

Yarn—
  60 g or 3 full skeins for each color of Anchor tapestry wool: Cream–8292, Blue–8744, Light Pink–8346, Dark Pink–8262

Essential Extras

Embroidery water-erasable pen
Fiberfill
Letter paper
Needle + thread
Roundheaded pins
Staple gun
Staple remover
Sewing machine
Yarn snips

SINCE SOME OF THE FABRIC WILL BE LEFT EXPOSED, WE RECOMMEND THAT YOU IRON YOUR FABRIC FIRST TO TAKE OUT ANY CREASES.

1. Assemble your stretcher bar frame. Stretch and staple-gun the fabric to your frame.

2. Transfer the template from page 126. Scale it up by using the instructions supplied. Using letter paper, draw and cut out the abstract shapes. Secure them in place, then, using the water-erasable embroidery pen, draw their outlines on the fabric.

3. Decide which shapes you will punch on the front and which you will punch on the back, and mark as necessary. Punching on both sides of the frame adds extra texture—so punch some of the shapes on the front of the frame in flat stitches to achieve more definition.

4. Follow the "Punch Needle Techniques" section on page 28 (4a).

    Snip away yarn tails to tidy up your work (4b).

5. Before removing it from the frame, mark the edges of the frame so you know where the design finishes. Use a ruler to draw a straight line to mark the sides.

6. Using fabric scissors, cut away the excess fabric, leaving a 1 in. seam allowance.

7. Lay out your finished work on top of the backing cloth and cut around your square cushion to create an identically sized backing cloth. Iron the backing cloth to take out any creases. Pin the right sides of the cushion and backing cloth together, leaving a gap of around 5 in. unpinned so you can turn your cushion to the right side later.

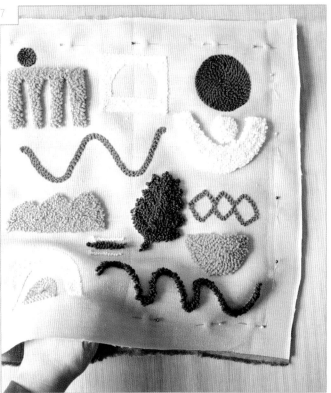

8. Using a sewing machine, sew straight lines around the rectangle, keeping in line with the markers that you made to mark the edge of the cushion (or your drawn ruler line).

9. Trim any excess seam allowance so you get a crisper edge before turning to the right side.

10. Turn to the right side and stuff with fiberfill, or use a cushion pad instead.

11. Sew the gap with ladder stitch.

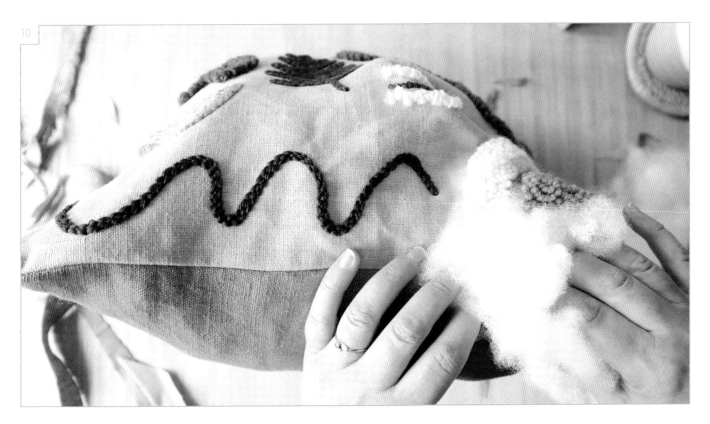

Small Rug

The Small Rug is the largest project in this book, but it's not overly technical to make, so it's in the intermediate-projects section. It's a project that you can really enjoy by taking your time by working on it over many evenings—or whenever you have some time to treat yourself to craft. It will give you a real sense of achievement when you complete this one, and we have ours proudly on display in front of our fireplace at home!

TOOLS AND MATERIALS

Frame—
1 pair of 24 in.
+ 1 pair of 36 in. canvas stretcher bars to make a rectangular frame

Punch needle fabric—
Natural linen

Punch needle tool—
Oxford size 10 regular punch needle

Yarn—
950 g (approximately) of rug yarn

Essential Extras
Clover clips
Ironing cloth
Letter paper
Marker pen
Needle + thread
Roundheaded pins
Scissors
Staple gun
Staple remover
Yarn snips

1. Assemble your stretcher bar frame. Stretch and staple-gun the fabric to your frame.

2. To transfer the design, you can cut out the abstract shapes, using letter paper, and draw around them, using a marker pen. If you press hard, this will transfer the marks through to the reverse of your fabric. If you want to use the template, you can scale the design up accordingly; follow the instructions on page 125.

3. Decide which colors you will use in which section, and also which areas you will punch on the front and which on the back; mark if necessary. Our rug uses both front and back loops.

4. Follow the "Punch Needle Techniques" section on pages 27–30 (4a).

   This Small Rug will take considerably longer than the previous projects, so take your time, don't hurry—just enjoy the rhythms of the craft. When it's complete, snip away the yarn tails to tidy up your work, and remove your work from the frame (4b).

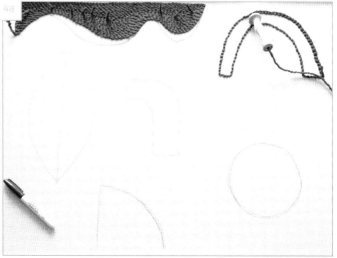

5a

5. Using fabric scissors, cut away the excess fabric, leaving a 1.5 in. seam allowance. Trim the edge of the corners diagonally (5a).

Press your rug flat by using a warm iron and protective cloth (5b).

5b

6. Working on a flat surface, fold the seam allowance over once, then again, to create the hem. Press the hem by using a cloth and iron (6a).

Using roundheaded pins, secure the hem in place. For the corners, fold the middle down first, then fold each corner into the middle. With roundheaded pins or clover clips, secure the corners in place (6b).

TIP: *Pull the hem as far back underneath as you can, so when your rug is lying flat the hem isn't visible.*

7. Using a darning needle and thread of your choice, sew the hem in place. This stage needs to be hand-sewn. Use whipstitch for the best results (7a).

Use your thumb as a space marker to get a consistent space between the stitches (7b).

For a neater finish, thread your last stitch back through the previous stitches (7c).

Cross-Body Bag

This Cross-Body Bag is practical and a great size for storing all your essentials in, while still being lightweight. It is stylish and makes your handmade bag your unique new fashion accessory to wear on everyday outings.

TOOLS AND MATERIALS

Backing fabric—
1 heavyweight organic cotton: for backing
+ 2 pieces of calico: for lining

Bag fastening—
1 18 mm magnetic fastening, optional

Frame—
2 pairs of 18 in. stretcher bar frames, making a square frame

Punch needle—
Size 10 regular Oxford punch needle

Punch needle fabric—
Open-weave white linen

Strap—
5 mm faux leather cord, cotton cord, or similar

Yarn—
300 g (approximately) of rug yarn

Essential Extras
Clover clips
Iron + towel
Marker pen
Scissors
Staple gun
Staple remover
Yarn needle
Yarn snips

1. Assemble your stretcher bar frame. Stretch and staple-gun the fabric to your frame.

2. Transfer the template from page 125. You can scale this up by using the instructions supplied, or draw the design freehand. Use a ruler to ensure that your top edge is straight.

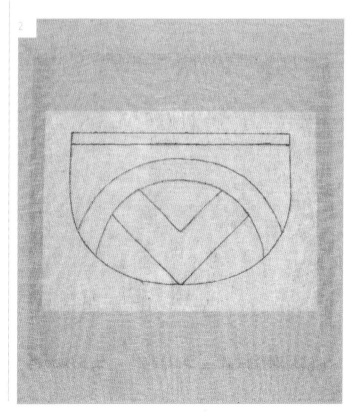

3. Decide which sections you will punch in flat stitches and which you will punch in loop stitches. This example project uses both.

4. Follow the "Punch Needle Techniques" section on pages 27–30. Once you have finished your design, snip away the yarn tails and remove it from the frame, carefully extracting the staples. Press the bag by using an iron and cloth. Using fabric scissors, cut away the excess cloth, leaving a 0.5 in. seam allowance. Add a thin line of Fray Check (or similar product) to the cut edge to prevent fraying.

5. Cut one piece of backing panel and two pieces of lining, remembering to include a 0.5 in. seam allowance. With the right sides facing, place the punch needle piece and back panel together; mark an opening approximately 1.5 in. down from the top panel to insert your straps. Mark this with a roundheaded pin (*see circle below*). Place the strap inside the bag and have the end of each strap come out through the side seam where your roundheaded pin is.

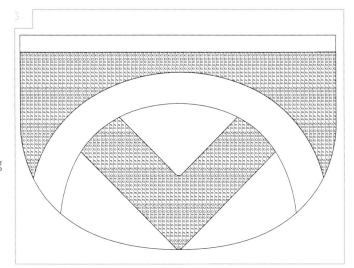

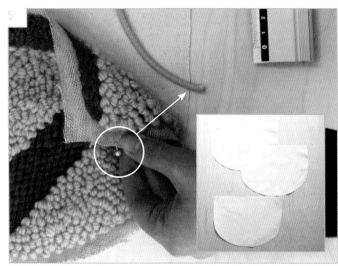

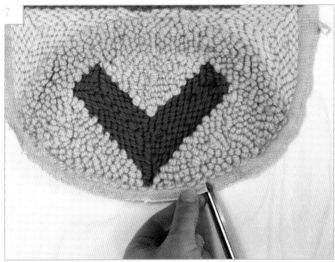

6. Use a clover clip to secure the strap ends in place. With your sewing machine and zipper foot, sew around the bag, leaving a 0.5 in. seam allowance.

TIP: *Try to sew as close to your punch needle stitches as possible. Remember to do a backstitch at the beginning and end of your machine stitch. Don't sew across your top opening!*

7. Clip-curve into your seam to create a smooth edge when the bag is folded out. This eliminates the bulk of the fabric and creates a smooth outer edge while still maintaining the curved shape.

   Turn right side out and, using an iron and cloth, press the seams out above where the straps have been inserted. This helps when inserting the lining. Finally, using the iron and cloth, press the curve of the bag, so this is nice and flat.

8. Place your lining pieces right sides facing together and pin—leaving a 0.5 in. seam allowance (8a).

   Remember to leave an opening of about 5 in. Stitch the seam by using a sewing machine (8b).

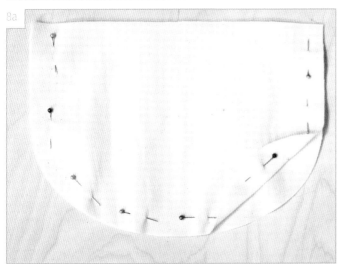

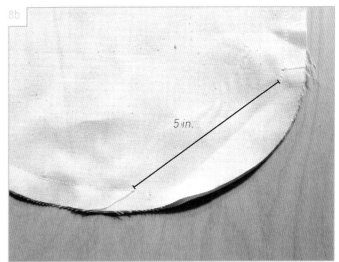

5 in.

9. Time to insert the magnetic fastening. Mark the center front of the back and front panels, then measure down from this about 2.5 in. Make sure that the fastening isn't too low, or you won't be able to fit many items in your bag. Place the center of your washer on the central marking you just made, and mark the slits on either side of the center. Fold a crease along this line and clip into the marked slits; make a small cut just big enough to insert the prongs of the snap-through. It's best to start small, since you can always make the slits bigger if needed.

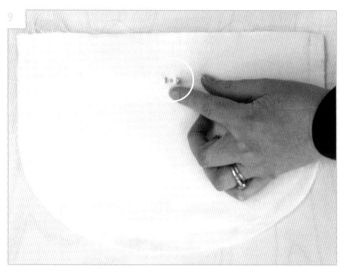

10. Place the prongs through the fabric: put the male snap on the front of the lining, and the female snap on the body of the bag. The snap side will be on the right side of your fabric, and the prongs on the reverse side. Place the metal washer over the prongs and fold the prongs as tightly as you can, making sure they're tight to the fabric. Open the prongs of the snap outward— for best results, use pliers—and press firmly against the surface. Alternatively, apply a thin piece of fusible fleece over the back of the magnetic snap once it has been installed. Repeat these steps for the other part. Clip-curve into the seam, then press the top of the seams out.

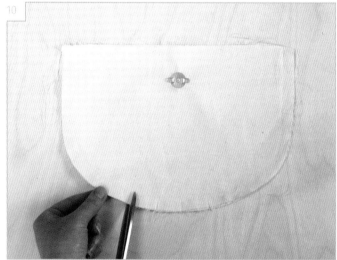

11. Now join the lining together with the main body of the bag. Take your punch needle work and turn it inside out. Insert the lining into the body, so the right sides are facing (11a).

Match up your pressed side seams—giving a nice flat edge to join. Pin or clip in place and, using your sewing machine with zipper foot, sew all the way around, as close to the punch needle edge as possible (11b–e).

11b

LINING, RIGHT SIDE OUT

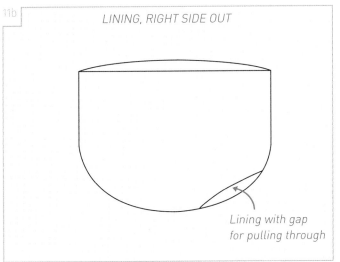

Lining with gap
for pulling through

11e

CLIP OR PIN IN PLACE, READY FOR STITCHING

Match up your side seams

Sew together using
your zipper foot,
staying as close to
the punch needle
edge as possible

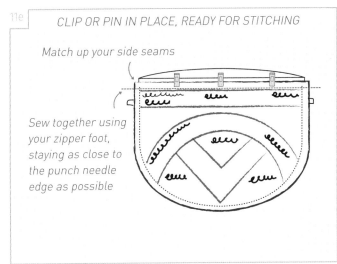

11c

BAG WITH WRONG SIDE OUT

Step 10—in detail—inserting lining

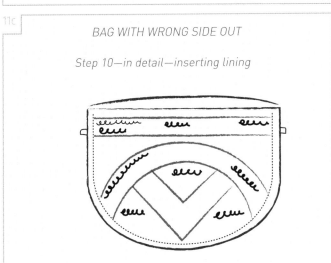

TIP: *Make sure that your bag strap is tucked safely inside and does not get caught up in sewing this last seam.*

12. Turn the bag back through to the right side, via the gap left in the lining. Give your bag a final press and sew up the opening in the lining, using invisible stitch. Now you're ready to take it out and about!

11d

BAG WITH WRONG SIDE OUT

Lining facing right
side out

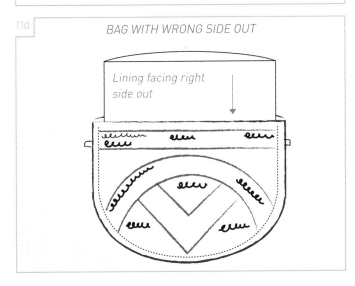

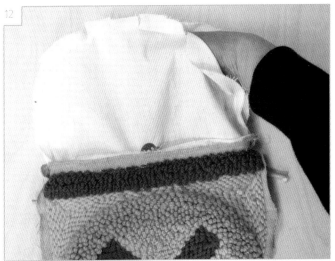

Tote Bag

This eye-catching Tote Bag makes a beautiful and sustainable fashion accessory for you to wear on days out. It's made from wool, organic cotton, felt, and wooden handles. In the future you won't need to worry about what to wear—this bag will make your outfit!

TOOLS AND MATERIALS

Backing cloth—
3 pieces of lining fabric*
(2 for sides + 1 for circular base)
+ 1 piece of felt for outer circular base
+ 1 piece of upholstery-weight organic cotton backing fabric

Frame—
2 pairs of 18 in. canvas stretcher bars to make a square frame

Punch needle—
Size 10 regular Oxford punch needle

Punch needle fabric—
Open-weave white linen

2 round wooden handles

Yarn—
600 g (approximately) of rug yarn

Essential Extras
Iron + towel
Marker pen
Scissors
Staple gun
Staple remover
Yarn needle
Yarn snips

1. Assemble the stretcher bar frame. Stretch and staple-gun the fabric to your frame.

2. Transfer the template from page 127. You can scale this up by using the instructions supplied. If you are confident, you can always draw the design freehand, but use a ruler to ensure that you have straight lines.

* **Note:** We sourced our backing fabric from a specialist haberdashery store and chose a fabric with a slight open weave, which makes it easier to pass the yarn needle through when it comes to attaching the wooden handle. You also need to consider a slightly open-weave fabric for the bag lining, since the yarn needle will also have to pass through this when whipstitching on the wooden handles.

3. Decide which sections you will punch in flat stitches and which you will punch in loop stitches: this example used both. Follow the "Punch Needle Techniques" section on pages 27–30. Once you have finished your design, snip away yarn tails to tidy up, and remove your work from the frame. Press well, using a warm iron and cloth. If you're not sewing your project straightaway, you could also leave your punch needle work under some heavy books to press flat.

4. Trim the fabric, leaving a 0.5 in. seam allowance, and apply Fray Check (or similar product) to the cut edge. Cut all your fabric pieces—one piece of backing cloth (because of the loose weave of this fabric, we also applied Fray Check here), plus two lining pieces and two circular bases—one in the same fabric as the lining, and one in felt for the main body.

5. Pin the lining pieces together, right sides facing. Sew down both sides, using a sewing machine, leaving a gap on one side for turning back to the right side. Press open the seams. Do the same with the punch needle front and backing, but there is no need to leave a gap.

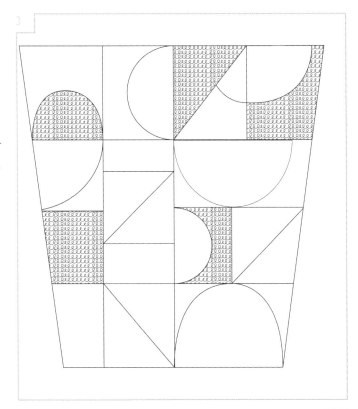

6. Attach the lining fabric with its matching circular base. Pin the right sides together, allowing a 0.5 in. seam allowance. Attaching the felt base to the main body is quite tricky because this is heavy material, so take your time to clip in place and then sew in tacking stitch to secure in place. The main body and the lining are ready now for sewing together.

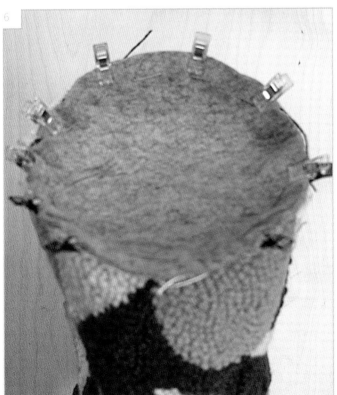

TIP: Use a contrasting thread color for this so you can easily remove it afterward. Once your pieces are in place, you can begin to machine-stitch very slowly and carefully.

7. Turn the punch needle piece inside out and insert the lining, so that right sides are together (7a).

Clip or pin the top seams together, matching up the side seams (7b).

Using your sewing machine, sew as close to the punch needle as possible. It's a good idea to do this slowly, using your zipper foot. Your fabric will want to slide out from under the presser foot, so do this as slowly as possible. Turn your bag through the gap in the lining so that the right sides are out (7c).

Give it another press.

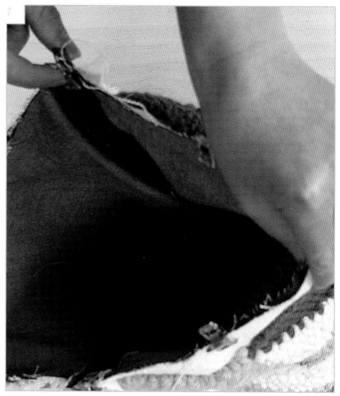

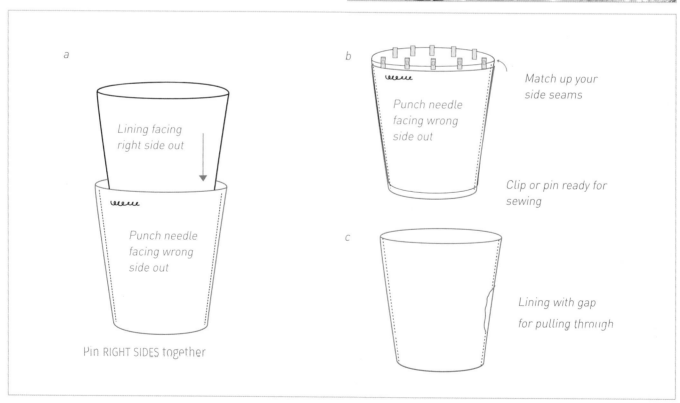

a

Lining facing right side out

Punch needle facing wrong side out

Pin RIGHT SIDES together

b

Punch needle facing wrong side out

Match up your side seams

Clip or pin ready for sewing

c

Lining with gap for pulling through

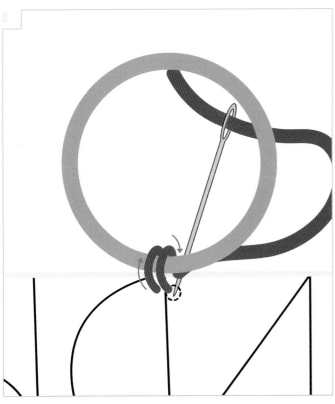

8. Attaching the wooden handles. To mark the center front, hold the handle in place and sew, using your yarn needle. It's a good idea to do a few stitches and double-check that the handle is fixed in the center.

Continue to whipstitch in place, keeping your yarn nice and tight. At the end, pass the tail of the yarn through a few of the loops, securing it in place before carefully trimming the end tail.

Repeat with the other handle. Attach it to the back panel and your project is now complete!

Templates

You can size the templates to any dimension you like.
We have provided you with the final size of the projects
we made for this book. However, you are free to size the
templates up or down to fit the space/size you want to fill.
For resizing, see page 26.

Large Wall Hanging
Finished artwork size:
19.6 in. high × 6.3 in. wide
(500 mm high × 160 mm wide)
SCALE UP BY 240%

Tech Cover

Finished artwork size:
7.8 in. wide × 10.6 in. high
(200 mm wide × 269 mm high)
SCALE UP BY 232%

Hexagon Cushion

Finished artwork size:
13.3 in. × 11.4 in. (337 mm × 291 mm)
SCALE UP BY 280%

Mini Wall Hanging

Finished artwork size:

7.4 in. × 11.8 in. (188 mm × 300 mm)

SCALE UP BY 164%

Large Wall Hanging

Finished artwork size:

8.7 in. × 30 in. (220 mm × 760 mm)

SCALE UP BY 417%

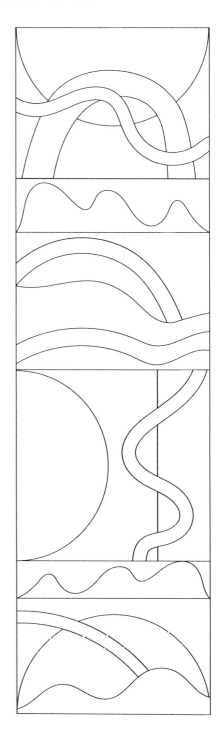

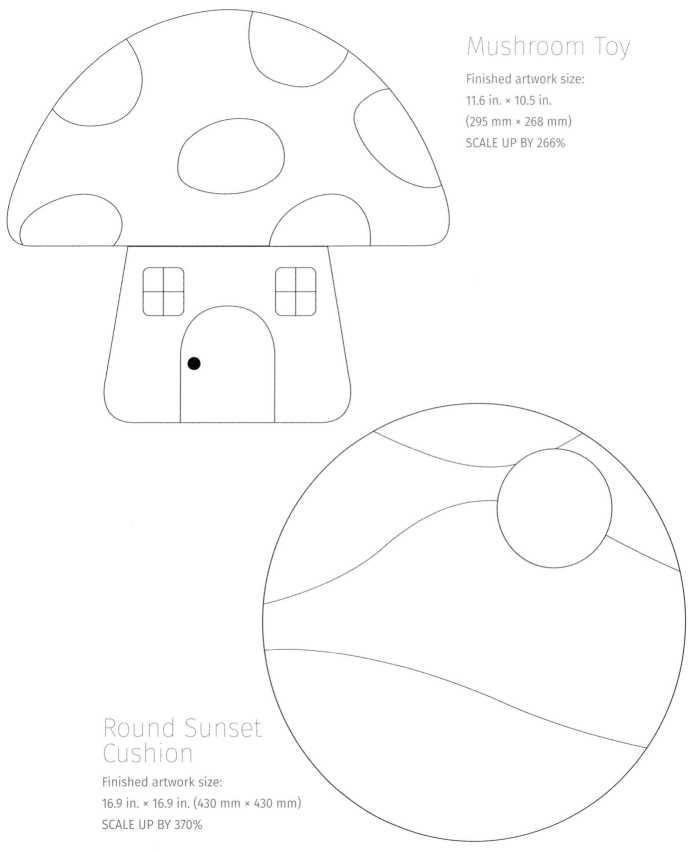

Mushroom Toy

Finished artwork size:
11.6 in. × 10.5 in.
(295 mm × 268 mm)
SCALE UP BY 266%

Round Sunset Cushion

Finished artwork size:
16.9 in. × 16.9 in. (430 mm × 430 mm)
SCALE UP BY 370%

Wall Storage Baskets

Finished artwork size:

7 in. wide × 8.4 in. high

(178 mm wide × 213mm high)

SCALE UP BY 204%

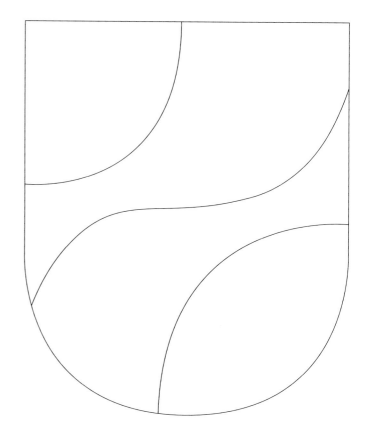

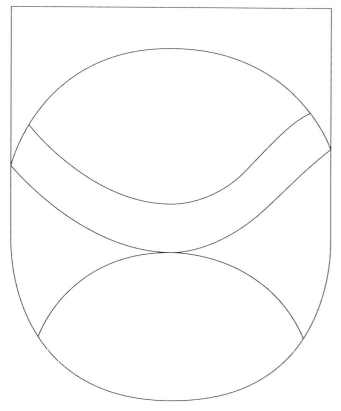

Small Rug

Finished artwork size:
25.7 in. × 19.6 in.
(655 mm × 500 mm)
SCALE UP BY 552%

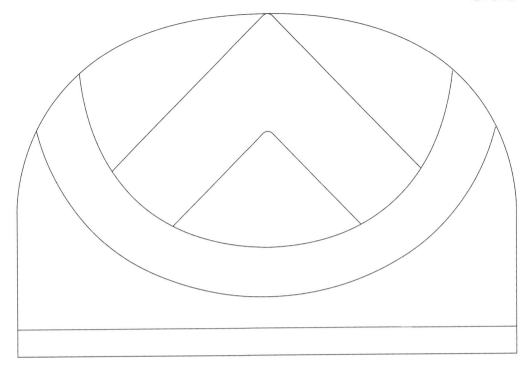

Patches

Actual size, various:
SCALE UP BY 184%

Cross-Body Bag

Finished artwork size: 9.4 in. wide × 6.2 in. high
(238 mm wide × 158mm high)
SCALE UP BY 203%

Square Abstract Cushion

Finished artwork size:
14.5 in. × 14.5 in.
(370 mm × 370 mm)
SCALE UP BY 327%

Turtle Toy

Finished artwork size:
15 in. wide
(384 mm wide)
SCALE UP BY 328%

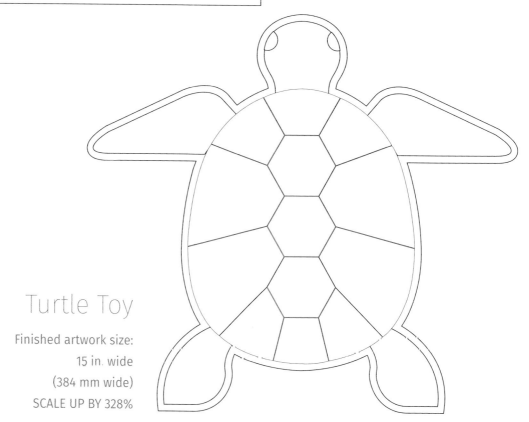

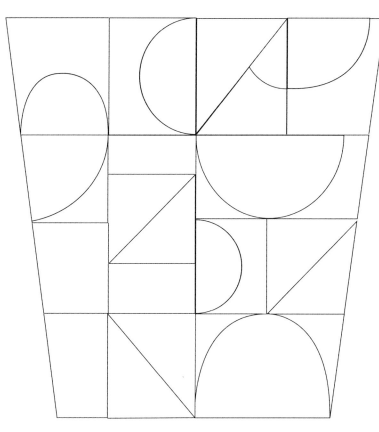

Tote Bag

Finished artwork size:
13.5 in. × 13.8 in. (widest point)
(344 mm × 353 mm)
SCALE UP BY 230%

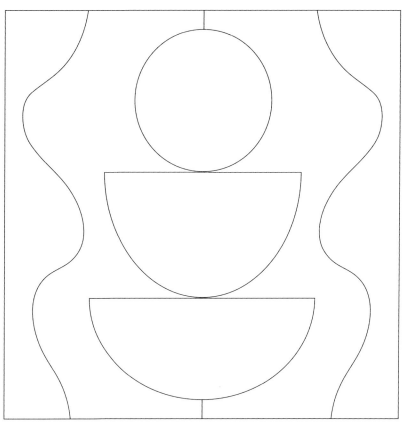

Trivet

Finished artwork size:
7.9 in. × 7.9 in. (203 mm × 203 mm)
SCALE UP BY 186%

About the Authors

Rachel and Siobhan started The Modern Crafter to combine designer skills with a passion for craft. Using Siobhan's design experience and Rachel's needlework skills, they have built a successful business and created modern, stylish projects that everyone can make.

The Modern Crafter has had their punch needle creations featured in *Mollie Makes* magazine and on the front cover of Not On The High Street's Christmas catalog. The Modern Crafter has also had their punch needle kits featured in *91 Magazine*. Together, Siobhan and Rachel have taught others the forgotten craft of punch needle through workshops and event demonstrations, and they are part of an encouraging crafting community on social media.

ACKNOWLEDGMENTS

Thank you to Jo Bryant at BlueRed Press for your encouragement and guiding us through making our first book. Believing in our brand and our work means so much to us. We've had so much fun!

Thank you to Diana Stainton for being a joy to work with and photographing our projects with such flair and understanding of our brand.

Thank you to Amy Oxford, Lavor Portugal, and our social media community for inspiring and encouraging us to keep on punch needling!

The biggest thank-you goes to our partners, Sam Burton and Matty Watt, and our family—we could not have achieved this without you by our sides.

To our beautiful children, Howie, Iris, and Elsbeth, we hope you will someday enjoy making these projects yourselves.

RESOURCES

Fabric, frames, wool, tools, and kits—*www.themoderncrafter.co.uk*

Other essentials extras were sourced via Ray Stitch, MacCulloch & Wallis, and LoveCrafts, and canvas bags from Hobbycraft.